ENGLISH HISTORICAL
DOCUMENTS
1906-1939

ENGLISH HISTORICAL DOCUMENTS
1906-1939

A Selection edited by

J. H. BETTEY M.A.

Senior History Master,
King Edward VI Grammar School,
Aston, Birmingham

ROUTLEDGE & KEGAN PAUL
LONDON AND HENLEY

First published 1967
by Routledge & Kegan Paul Limited
39 Store Street
London WC1E 7DD and
Broadway House, Newtown Road
Henley-on-Thames
Oxon. RG9 1EN

Reprinted 1974, 1976, 1978 and 1980

Printed in Great Britain by
Redwood Burn Limited
Trowbridge & Esher

ISBN 0 7100 2883 0

Contents

COMMONWEALTH

INTERNATIONAL DISPUTES

Preface

The purpose of the following selection of documents is to provide in a convenient form extracts from important and significant documents of the years 1906 to 1939. In a period so crowded with events and so rich in historical material the problem of selection is difficult; inevitably, in a work of this length there are many important topics which are not represented. However, extracts have been included from a number of different types of contemporary documents, making it possible for students to read for themselves documents which are frequently referred to by writers on this period but which are not always easily accessible. The introductory notes to each extract or group of extracts are intended merely to sketch the background and do not attempt to give the history of each of the incidents mentioned.

J. H. B.

Acknowledgements

Thanks are due to the following for kind permission to print extracts included in this selection:

The Beaverbrook Foundations; D. Lloyd George, *War Memoirs*, Nicholson and Watson, London, 1933–6; J. M. Dent and Sons: *Sir Douglas Haig's Despatches*, ed. J. H. Boraston, London, 1919; Eyre and Spottiswoode: *The Private Papers of Douglas Haig*, ed. R. Blake, London, 1952; Rupert Hart-Davis: G. M. Young, *Stanley Baldwin*, London, 1952; Her Majesty's Stationery Office: Government Acts, Reports, Parliamentary Debates, *Hansard* and The *British Gazette*; the Labour Party: the Report of the Thirty-fifth Annual Conference 1935; the Statesman and Nation Publishing Co.: the *New Statesman*, 29 August 1931; Odhams Books: W. S. Churchill, *The World Crisis*, Thornton Butterworth, London, 1923; Odhams Press: the *Daily Herald*, 24 May 1926; Oxford University Press: *Speeches and Documents on International Affairs*, ed. A. B. Keith, London, 1938, and H. W. V. Temperley, *The History of the Peace Conference of Paris*, London, 1920–4; The Times Publishing Company: *The Times*, 31 July, 30 November 1909, 10 August 1911, 26 October 1923, 6 May 1926, 25 August 1931, 12 September 1935; the Trades Union Congress: *The British Worker*, 7 May 1926, Memorandum on the General Strike 1 May 1926 in *Trade Union Documents*, ed. W. Milne-Bailey, G. Bell and Sons, London, 1929, and the Samuel Memorandum 10 May 1926.

The Beginning of the Welfare State

1. OLD AGE PENSIONS ACT 1908

The Budget of 1908 had been prepared by Asquith, who was Chancellor of the Exchequer until April, when he succeeded Campbell-Bannerman as Prime Minister. Lloyd George then became Chancellor of the Exchequer, but Asquith introduced the Budget in the House of Commons on 7 May 1908. The most important feature of the Budget was that it provided the sum of £1,200,000 to finance a scheme of non-contributory Old Age Pensions to start on 1 January 1909. The proposals were then embodied in the Old Age Pensions Act.

The scheme was a very narrow one, for it applied only to the very poor. The pensions were not to start until the age of 70 and were not more than five shillings a week or seven shillings and sixpence for a married couple. The importance of the Act lay, not in the small pension that was granted, but in the fact that it was a new departure and that it began a policy of relieving poverty by direct payments from the State. It therefore paved the way for much of the future development of the Welfare State. The main parts of the Act are given in the following extract.

OLD AGE PENSIONS ACT 1908

(Public General Acts 8 Ed 7 c 40)

An Act to provide for Old Age Pensions. (1 August 1908)

Be it enacted by the King's most Excellent Majesty, by and with the advice and consent of the Lords Spiritual and Temporal, and Commons, in this present Parliament assembled, and by the authority of the same, as follows:

1.   (1) Every person in whose case the conditions laid down by this Act for the receipt of an old age pension (in this Act referred to as statutory conditions) are fulfilled, shall be entitled

1

to receive such a pension under this Act so long as those conditions continue to be fulfilled, and so long as he is not disqualified under this Act for the receipt of the pension.

(2) An old age pension under this Act shall be at the rate set forth in the schedule to this Act.

(3) The sums required for the payment of old age pensions under this Act shall be paid out of moneys provided by Parliament.

(4) The receipt of an old age pension under this Act shall not deprive the pensioner of any franchise, right, or privilege or subject him to any disability.

2. The statutory conditions for the receipt of an old age pension by any person are

(1) The person must have attained the age of seventy.

(2) The person must satisfy the pension authorities that for at least twenty years up to the date of the receipt of any sum on account of a pension he has been a British subject, and has had his residence, as defined by regulations under this Act, in the United Kingdom.

(3) The person must satisfy the pension authorities that his yearly means as calculated under this Act do not exceed thirty-one pounds ten shillings.

3. (1) A person shall be disqualified for receiving or continuing to receive an old age pension under this Act, notwithstanding the fulfilment of the statutory conditions—

(a) While he is in receipt of any poor relief (other than relief excepted under this provision), and, until the thirty-first day of December nineteen hundred and ten unless Parliament otherwise determines, if he has at any time since the first day of January nineteen hundred and eight received or hereafter receives, any such relief: Provided that for the purposes of this provision—

(i) any medical or surgical assistance (including food or comforts) supplied by or on the recommendation of a medical officer; or

(ii) any relief given to any person by means of the maintenance of any dependant of that person in any lunatic asylum, infirmary, or hospital, or the payment of any expenses of the burial of a dependant; or

(iii) any relief (other than medical or surgical assistance or relief herein-before specifically exempted) which by law is expressly declared not to be a disqualification for registration as a parliamentary elector, or a reason for depriving any person of any franchise, right, or privilege;

shall not be considered as poor relief:

(b) If, before he becomes entitled to a pension, he has habitually failed to work according to his ability, opportunity, and need, for the maintenance or benefit of himself and those legally dependent upon him:

Provided that a person shall not be disqualified under this paragraph if he has continuously for ten years up to attaining the age of sixty, by means of payments to friendly, provident or other societies, or trade unions, or other approved steps, made such provision against old age, sickness, infirmity, or want or loss of employment as may be recognised as proper provision for the purpose by regulations under this Act, and any such provision, when made by the husband in the case of a married couple living together, shall as respects any right of the wife to a pension, be treated as provision made by the wife as well as by the husband:

(c) While he is detained in any asylum within the meaning of the Lunacy Act, 1890, or while he is being maintained in any place as a pauper or criminal lunatic:

(d) During the continuance of any period of disqualification arising or imposed in pursuance of this section in consequence of conviction for an offence.

(2) Where a person has been before the passing of this Act, or is after the passing of this Act, convicted of any offence, and ordered to be imprisoned without the option of a fine or to suffer any greater punishment, he shall be disqualified for receiving or continuing to receive an old age pension under this Act while he is detained in prison in consequence of the order, and for a further period of ten years after the date on which he is released from prison.

(3) Where a person of sixty years of age or upwards having been convicted before any court is liable to have a detention order made against him under the Inebriates Act, 1898, and is not necessarily, by virtue of the provisions of this Act, disqualified for receiving or continuing to receive an old age pension under this Act, the court may, if they think fit, order that the

person convicted be so disqualified for such period, not exceeding ten years, as the Court direct.

4. (1) In calculating the means of a person for the purpose of this Act account shall be taken of—

(a) the income which that person may reasonably expect to receive during the succeeding year in cash, excluding any sums receivable on account of an old age pension under this Act, that income, in the absence of other means for ascertaining the income, being taken to be the income actually received during the preceding year;

(b) the yearly value of any advantage accruing to that person from the use or enjoyment of any property belonging to him which is personally used or enjoyed by him;

(c) the yearly income which might be expected to be derived from any property belonging to that person which, though capable of investment or profitable use is not so invested or profitably used by him; and

(d) the yearly value of any benefit or privilege enjoyed by that person.

(2) In calculating the means of a person being one of a married couple living together in the same house, the means shall not in any case be taken to be a less amount than half the total means of the couple.

(3) If it appears that any person has directly or indirectly deprived himself of any income or property in order to qualify himself for the receipt of an old age pension, or for the receipt of an old age pension at a higher rate than that to which he would otherwise be entitled under this Act, that income or the yearly value of that property shall, for the purposes of this section, be taken to be part of the means of that person.

5. (1) An old age pension under this Act, subject to any directions of the Treasury in special cases, shall be paid weekly in advance in such manner and subject to such conditions as to identification or otherwise as the Treasury direct.

(2) A pension shall commence to accrue on the first Friday after the claim for the pension has been allowed, or, in the case of a claim provisionally allowed, on the first Friday after the day on which the claimant becomes entitled to receive the pension.

*   *   *

9. (2) If it is found at any time that a person has been in receipt of an old age pension under this Act while the statutory conditions were not fulfilled in his case or while he was disqualified for receiving the pension, he or, in the case of his death, his personal representative, shall be liable to repay to the Treasury any sums paid to him in respect of the pension while the statutory conditions were not fulfilled or while he was disqualified for receiving the pension, and the amount of those sums may be recovered as a debt due to the Crown.

* * *

12. (1) A person shall not be entitled to the receipt of an old age pension under this Act until the first day of January nineteen hundred and nine and no such pension shall begin to accrue until that day.

(2) This Act may be cited as the Old Age Pensions Act, 1908.

SCHEDULE

Means of Pensioner	Rate of Pension Per Week	
Where the yearly means of the Pensioner as calculated under this Act—	s.	d.
do not exceed £21	5	0
Exceed £21, but do not exceed £23 12s. 6d. ..	4	0
Exceed £23 12s. 6d., but do not exceed £26 5s.	3	0
Exceed £26 5s., but do not exceed £28 17s. 6d.	2	0
Exceed £28 17s. 6d., but do not exceed £31 10s.	1	0
Exceed £31 10s.	No pension	

5

2. NATIONAL INSURANCE ACT 1911

The National Insurance Act was a most important and far-reaching measure of social legislation. It was a contributory scheme designed to insure the whole working population against sickness and many workers against unemployment. It was designed to provide support in times of distress for great numbers of people who otherwise had no resource but the Poor Law.

The Bill was introduced into the House of Commons on 4 May 1911 by Lloyd George. Lloyd George had studied the operation of a similar scheme in Germany, and he had been chiefly responsible for drawing up the Bill. The measure encountered severe opposition both in Parliament and in the country. It was attacked because of the infringement of liberty and the regimentation which it was said to involve, and because of the fears of the medical profession and of the voluntary insurance societies. Lloyd George showed great skill in guiding the Bill through Parliament and in securing the co-operation of the doctors and of the voluntary insurance societies. The Act came into operation on 15 July 1912 and those insured became eligible for medical benefit six months later.

This is an extremely long and detailed Act and only some of its main provisions are given here.

NATIONAL INSURANCE ACT 1911
(Public General Acts 1 and 2 Geo 5 c 55)

An Act to provide for Insurance against Loss of Health and Cure of Sickness and for Insurance against Unemployment, and for purposes incidental thereto. (16 December 1911)

Be it enacted . . . as follows:

Part I: National Health Insurance

Insured Persons
1. Subject to the provisions of this Act, all persons of the age of sixteen and upwards who are employed within the meaning of this Part of this Act shall be, and any such persons who are not so employed but who possess the qualifications herein-after mentioned may be, insured in manner provided in this Part of this Act, and all persons so insured (in this Act called 'insured

persons') shall be entitled in the manner and subject to the conditions provided in this Act to the benefits in respect of health insurance and prevention of sickness conferred by this Part of this Act . . .

2. Where any person employed within the meaning of this Part of this Act proves that he is either—

(a) in receipt of any pension or income of the annual value of twenty-six pounds or upwards not dependent upon his personal exertions; or

(b) ordinarily and mainly dependent for his livelihood upon some other person;

he shall be entitled to a certificate exempting him from the liability to become or to continue to be insured under this Part of this Act. . . .

Contributions

3. Except as otherwise provided by this Act, the funds for providing the benefits conferred by this Part of this Act and defraying the expenses of the administration of those benefits shall be derived as to seven-ninths (or, in the case of women, three-fourths) thereof from contributions made by or in respect of the contributors by themselves or their employers, and as to the remaining two-ninths (or, in the case of women, one quarter) thereof from moneys provided by Parliament.

4. (1) The Contributions payable in respect of employed contributors shall be at the rate specified in Part 1 of the Second Schedule to the Act . . . and shall comprise contributions by the contributors and contributions by their employers at the rates specified in that Part of that schedule and shall be payable at weekly or other prescribed intervals. . . .

(2) The employer shall, in the first instance, pay both the contributions payable by himself (in this Act referred to as the employers contributions), and also on behalf of the employed contributor the contributions payable by such contributor, and shall be entitled to recover from the contributor by deduction from his wages or otherwise the amount of the contributions so paid by him on behalf of the contributor. . . .

(3) Contributions in respect of employed contributors shall cease to be payable on their attaining the age of seventy. . . .

Benefits

8. (1) Subject to the provisions of this Act, the benefits conferred by this Part of this Act upon insured persons are—

(a) Medical treatment and attendance, including the provision of proper and sufficient medicines, and such medical surgical appliances as may be prescribed by regulations to be made by the Insurance Commissioners (in this Act called 'medical benefit');

(b) Treatment in sanatoria or other institutions or otherwise when suffering from tuberculosis, or such other diseases as the Local Government Board with the approval of the Treasury may appoint (in this Act called 'Sanatorium benefit');

(c) Periodical payments whilst rendered incapable of work by some specific disease or by bodily or mental disablement, of which notice has been given, commencing from the fourth day after being so rendered incapable of work, and continuing for a period not exceeding twenty-six weeks (in this Act called 'sickness benefit');

(d) In the case of the disease or disablement continuing after the determination of sickness benefit, periodical payments so long as so rendered incapable of work by the disease or disablement (in this Act called 'disablement benefit');

(e) Payment in the case of the confinement of the wife or, where the child is a posthumous child, of the widow of an insured person, or of any woman who is an insured person, of a sum of thirty shillings (in this Act called 'maternity benefit');

(f) In the case of persons entitled under this Part of this Act to any of the further benefits mentioned in Part II of the Fourth Schedule to this Act (in this Act called 'additional benefits') such of those benefits as they may be entitled to. ...

(3) In the case of insured persons who have attained the age of seventy, the right to sickness benefit and disablement benefit shall cease. . . .

Part II: Unemployment Insurance

84. Every workman who, having been employed in a trade ... is unemployed, and in whose case the conditions laid down by this Part of this Act (in this Act referred to as 'statutory con-

ditions') are fulfilled, shall be entitled, subject to the provisions of this Part of this Act, to receive payments (in this Act referred to as 'unemployment benefit') at weekly or other prescribed intervals at such rates and for such periods as are authorised by or under the Seventh Schedule to this Act, so long as those conditions continue to be fulfilled, and so long as he is not disqualified under this Act for the receipt of unemployment benefit.

Provided that unemployment benefit shall not be paid in respect of any period of unemployment which occurs during the six months following the commencement of this Act.

85. (1) The sums required for the payment of unemployment benefit under this Act shall be derived partly from contributions by workmen in the insured trades and partly from contributions by employers of such workmen and partly from moneys provided by Parliament.

(2) Subject to the provisions of this Part of this Act, every workman employed within the United Kingdom in an insured trade, and every employer of such workmen, shall be liable to pay contributions at the rates specified in the Eighth Schedule to the Act.

(3) Except where the regulations under this Part of this Act otherwise prescribe, the employer shall, in the first instance, be liable to pay both the contribution payable by himself, and also on behalf of and to the exclusion of the workman, the contribution payable by such workman, and subject to such regulations, shall be entitled, notwithstanding the provisions of any Act or any contract to the contrary, to recover from the workman by deductions from the workman's wages or from any other payment due from him to the workman the amount of the contributions so paid by him on behalf of the workman.

(4) Notwithstanding any contract to the contrary, the employer shall not be entitled to deduct from the wages of or other payment due to the workman, or otherwise recover from the workman by any legal process the contributions payable by the employer himself. . . .

(6) A contribution shall be made in each year out of moneys provided by Parliament equal to one-third of the total contributions received from employers and workmen during that year, and the sums to be contributed in any year shall be paid

in such manner and at such times as the Treasury may determine.

86. The statutory conditions for the receipt of unemployment benefit by any workman are—

(1) that he proves that he has been employed as a workman in an insured trade in each of not less than twenty-six separate calendar weeks in the preceding five years;

(2) that he has made application for unemployment benefit in the prescribed manner, and proves that since the date of application he has been continuously unemployed;

(3) that he is capable of work but unable to obtain suitable employment;

(4) that he has not exhausted his right to unemployment benefit under this Part of this Act:

Provided that a workman shall not be deemed to have failed to fulfil the statutory conditions by reason only that he has declined—

(a) an offer of employment in a situation vacant in consequence of a stoppage of work due to a trade dispute; or

(b) an offer of employment in the district where he was last ordinarily employed at a rate of wage lower, or on conditions less favourable, than those which he habitually obtained in his usual employment in that district, or would have obtained had he continued to be so employed; or

(c) an offer of employment in any other district at a rate of wage lower or on conditions less favourable than those generally observed in such district by agreement between associations of employers and of workmen, or, failing any such agreement, than those generally recognised in such district by good employers.

87. (1) A workman who has lost employment by reason of a stoppage of work which was due to a trade dispute at the factory, workshop, or other premises at which he was employed, shall be disqualified for receiving unemployment benefit so long as the stoppage of work continues, except in a case where he has, during the stoppage of work, become bonâ fide employed elsewhere in an insured trade. . . .

(2) A workman who loses employment through misconduct or who voluntarily leaves his employment without just cause

shall be disqualified for receiving unemployment benefit for a period of six weeks from the date when he so lost employment.

(3) A workman shall be disqualified for receiving unemployment benefit whilst he is an inmate of any prison or any workhouse or other institution supported wholly or partly out of public funds and whilst he is resident temporarily or permanently outside the United Kingdom.

(4) A workman shall be disqualified for receiving unemployment benefit while he is in receipt of any sickness or disablement benefit or any disablement allowance under Part I of this Act. . . .

SCHEDULES: FIRST SCHEDULE

PART I

Employments within the meaning of Part I of this Act relating to Health Insurance

(a) Employment in the United Kingdom under any contract of service or apprenticeship, written or oral, whether expressed or implied, and whether the employed person is paid by the employer or by some other person, and whether under one or more employers, and whether paid by time or by the piece. . . .

PART II

Exceptions

(a) Employment in the naval or military service of the Crown . . .

(b) Employment under the Crown or any local or other public authority where the Insurance Commissioners certify that the terms of the employment are such as to secure provision in respect of sickness and disablement on the whole not less favourable than the corresponding benefits conferred by Part I of this Act

(c) Employment as a clerk or other salaried official in the service of a railway or other statutory company . . . where the Insurance Commissioners certify that the terms of employment . . . are such as to secure provision in respect of sickness and disablement, on the whole, not less favourable than the corresponding benefits conferred by Part I of this Act. . . .

(g) Employment otherwise than by way of manual labour and at a rate of remuneration exceeding in value one hundred and sixty pounds a year. . . .

SECOND SCHEDULE: Rates of Contribution under Part I of this Act relating to Health Insurance

PART I

Employed Rate

In the case of men	7d. a week
In the case of women	6d. a week

Contributions by Employers and Employed Contributors

To be paid by the employers	3d. a week
To be paid by the contributor	Men 4d. a week
	Women 3d. a week

*   *   *

FOURTH SCHEDULE: Benefits under Part I of this Act relating to Health Insurance

PART I

Rates of Benefits: Table A   *Ordinary Rates*
Sickness Benefit: for men, the sum of 10s. a week throughout the whole period of twenty-six weeks; for women, the sum of 7s. 6d. a week throughout the whole period of twenty-six weeks. Disablement benefit: the sum of 5s. a week for men and women alike.

*   *   *

SEVENTH SCHEDULE

Rates and Periods of Unemployment Benefit
In respect of each week following the first week of any period of unemployment, seven shillings, or such other rates as may be prescribed either generally or for any particular trade or any branch thereof:
Provided that, in the case of a workman under the age of eighteen, no unemployment benefit shall be paid while the workman is below the age of seventeen, and while the workman is of the age of seventeen or upwards but below the age of

eighteen, unemployment benefit shall only be paid at half the rate at which it would be payable if the workman was above the age of eighteen.

No workman shall receive unemployment benefit for more than fifteen or such other number of weeks as may be prescribed either generally or for any particular trade or branch thereof within any period of twelve months, or in respect of any period less than one day.

No workman shall receive more unemployment benefit than in the proportion of one week's benefit for every five contributions paid by him under this Act. . . .

EIGHTH SCHEDULE : Contributions for the purposes of Part II of this Act relating to Unemployment Insurance

Rates of Contribution from Workmen and Employers
From every workman employed in an insured trade for every week he is so employed 2½d
From every employer by whom one or more workmen are employed in an insured trade, in respect of each workman, for every week he is so employed 2½d

The Constitutional Crisis

3. THE CONTROVERSY OVER THE BUDGET PROPOSALS 1909

The conflict between the House of Lords and the House of Commons had been growing in intensity during the years 1906 to 1909, as the Lords rejected more and more of the proposals of the Liberal Government. It came to a head with Lloyd George's Budget of 1909. The Budget, which was introduced in April 1909, was designed to increase the revenue of the Government in order to finance measures of social reform and to provide for a considerable growth in expenditure on armaments. The result was a highly controversial Budget which contained a number of new proposals and increased existing taxes. It provoked intense attack from the Conservative opposition in the Commons and from the House of Lords. The main objections of the Lords were directed against the proposals to tax the profits derived by landowners from the increased value of their land, from site values and leaseholds, and from undeveloped land and mineral rights. These proposals would involve compulsory registration and valuation of land and were thought by some to be the beginning of an attack on the private ownership of land.

During the Summer of 1909, whilst the Budget was being debated by the Commons, Lloyd George delivered a number of speeches in various parts of the country in which he justified his proposals and ridiculed those who opposed them. The best known of these speeches was delivered at the Edinburgh Castle public house at Limehouse in the East End of London on 30 July 1909. This speech became notorious for the vigour of its attack on the rich and its threats of even more severe government action against them, including land nationalisation.

(Note: *The Times* throughout this report hyphenates the name

Lloyd George. He himself did not hyphenate it and it is normally spelt without a hyphen.)

The Finance Bill 1909: The bitterness of Lloyd George's attacks and the scorn and ridicule which he poured upon his opponents served only to make his critics in the House of Lords more determined. The Budget proposals passed the House of Commons on 4 November 1909 by 379 votes to 149, but were rejected by the House of Lords on 30 November by 350 votes to 75.

It was generally accepted that the House of Lords did not have the power to amend bills dealing with finance. The question of whether or not they had the power to reject such a Bill outright was a very difficult one. Rejection of the Budget was certain to give rise to a very fierce struggle between the Lords and the Commons and to raise the whole problem of the position of the House of Lords in the Constitution.

Lord Lansdowne was one of the foremost of those who urged that the Budget should be rejected by the Lords, and an extract from his speech is given below. Other aspects of the argument are given in the extracts from *The Times* leading article and from the speech made by Asquith in the House of Commons after the rejection of the Budget by the Lords.

Asquith's resolution of 2 December was carried in the House of Commons by 349 votes to 134 and a General Election was thus made inevitable. It was to require two General Elections and a very fierce and prolonged political contest before the crisis was ended in 1911 with the passing of the Parliament Act.

(3a) Extract from Mr. Lloyd George's speech at Limehouse 30 July 1909 as reported in The Times *31 July 1909*

Under the auspices of the Budget League Mr Lloyd-George, Chancellor of the Exchequer, addressed a very large meeting in the Edinburgh Castle, Limehouse, last night. The building was crowded with an audience which numbered about 4,000.

A large body of police was on duty outside the building. The suffragists mustered in considerable strength and endeavoured to get admission to the hall. They were, however, repulsed by the officers who were charged with the duty of keeping the doors. Mr Lloyd-George, who was accompanied by Mrs Lloyd-George, had an enthusiastic reception on reaching the platform.

Whilst the cheers which greeted him were in progress a man who wore the suffragist colours climbed up the pillar supporting the roof and tied himself to it. He was soon followed by half-a-dozen stewards. One climbed up to him, and, pulling out a knife, cut the straps and ropes by which the individual had fastened himself. They then hauled the man down among the great crowd of stewards collected around the base of the pillar. It was soon apparent that several sympathisers with the suffragists had ranged themselves in the particular quarter of the hall, and six of them were promptly removed. Though the stewards apparently used no more violence than was necessary, each man received a rough handling at the hands of the members of the audience whom he passed, and one, it was stated, had to be taken to hospital.

Mr Lloyd-George, who on rising had an enthusiastic reception, said, 'A few months ago a meeting was held not far from this hall, in the heart of the City of London, demanding that the Government should launch out and run into enormous expenditure on the Navy. That meeting ended up with a resolution promising that those who passed that resolution would give financial support to the Government in their undertaking. There have been two or three meetings held in the City of London since (laughter and cheers), attended by the same class of people, but not ending up with a resolution promising to pay. (Laughter.) On the contrary, we are spending the money, but they won't pay. (Laughter.) What has happened since to alter their tone? Simply that we have sent in the bill. (Laughter and cheers.) We started our four Dreadnoughts. They cost eight millions of money. We promised them four more; they cost another eight millions. Somebody has got to pay, and these gentlemen say, "Perfectly true; somebody has got to pay, but we would rather that somebody were somebody else." (Laughter.) We started building; we wanted money to pay for the building; so we sent the hat round. (Laughter.) We sent it round amongst the workmen (hear, hear), and the miners of Derbyshire (loud cheers) and Yorkshire, the weavers of High Peak (cheers) and the Scotchmen of Dumfries (cheers), who, like all their countrymen, know the value of money. (Laughter.) They all brought in their coppers. We went round Belgravia, but there has been such a howl ever since that it has completely deafened us.'

Old Age Pensions
'But they say "It is not so much the Dreadnoughts we object to, it is the pensions." (Hear, hear.) If they object to pensions, why did they promise them? (Cheers.) They won elections on the strength of their promises. It is true they never carried them out. (Laughter.) Deception is always a pretty contemptible vice, but to deceive the poor is the meanest of all crimes. (Cheers.) But they say, "When we promised pensions we meant pensions at the expense of the people for whom they were provided. We simply meant to bring in a Bill to compel workmen to contribute to their own pensions." (Laughter.) If that is what they meant, why did they not say so? (Cheers.) The Budget, as your chairman has already so well reminded you, is introduced not merely for the purpose of raising barren taxes, but taxes that are fertile taxes, taxes that will bring forth fruit— the security of the country which is paramount in the minds of all. The provision for the aged and deserving poor—it was time it was done. (Cheers.) It is rather a shame for a rich country like ours—probably the richest country in the world, if not the richest the world has ever seen—that it should allow those who have toiled all their days to end in penury and possibly starvation. (Hear, hear.) It is rather hard that an old workman should have to find his way to the gates of the tomb, bleeding and footsore, through the brambles and thorns of poverty. (Cheers.) We cut a new path through it (cheers) an easier one, a pleasanter one, through fields of waving corn. We are raising money to pay for the new road (cheers), aye, and to widen it so that 200,000 paupers shall be able to join in the march. (Cheers.) There are many in the country blessed by Providence with great wealth, and if there are amongst them men who grudge out of their riches a fair contribution towards the less fortunate of their fellow-countrymen they are shabby rich men. (Cheers.) We propose to do more by means of the Budget. We are raising money to provide against the evils and the sufferings that follow from unemployment. (Cheers.) We are raising money for the purpose of assisting our great friendly societies to provide for the sick and the widows and orphans. We are providing money to

17

enable us to develop the resources of our own land. (Cheers.) I do not believe any fair-minded man would challenge the justice and the fairness of the objects which we have in view in raising this money.'

*　　*　　*

'The other day, at the great Tory meeting held at the Cannon-street Hotel, they had blazoned on the walls, "We protest against the Budget in the name of democracy—(loud laughter)—liberty, and justice." Where does the democracy come in in this landed system? Where is the justice in all these transactions? We claim that the tax we impose on land is fair, just, and moderate. (Cheers.) They go on threatening that if we proceed they will cut down their benefactions and discharge labour. What kind of labour? (A voice, "Hard labour," and laughter.) What is the labour they are going to choose for dismissal? Are they going to threaten to devastate rural England while feeding themselves, and dressing themselves? Are they going to reduce their gamekeepers? That would be sad! (Laughter.) The agricultural labourer and the farmer might then have some part of the game which they fatten with their labour. But what would happen to you in the season? No week-end shooting with the Duke of Norfolk for any of us! (Laughter.) But that is not the kind of labour that they are going to cut down. They are going to cut down productive labour—builders and gardeners—and they are going to ruin their property so that it shall not be taxed. All I can say is this—the ownership of land is not merely an enjoyment, it is a stewardship. (Cheers.) It has been reckoned as such in the past, and if they cease to discharge their functions, the security and defence of the country, looking after the broken in their villages and neighbourhoods—then those functions which are part of the traditional duties attached to the ownership of land and which have given to it its title—if they cease to discharge those functions, the time will come to reconsider the conditions under which land is held in this country. (Loud cheers.) No country, however rich, can permanently afford to have quartered upon its revenue a class which declines to do the duty which it was called upon to perform. (Hear, hear.) And, therefore, it is one of the prime duties of statesmanship to investigate those conditions. But I do not believe it.

They have threatened and menaced like that before. They have seen it is not to their interest to carry out these futile menaces. They are now protesting against paying their fair share of the taxation of the land, and they are doing so by saying: "You are burdening the community; you are putting burdens upon the people which they cannot bear." Ah! they are not thinking of themselves. (Laughter.) Noble souls! (Laughter.) It is not the great dukes they are feeling for, it is the market gardener (laughter), it is the builder, and it was, until recently, the small holder. (Hear, hear.) In every debate in the House of Commons they said: "We are not worrying for ourselves. We can afford it with our broad acres; but just think of the little man who has only got a few acres"; and we were so very impressed with this tearful appeal that at last we said, "We will leave him out." (Cheers.) And I almost expected to see Mr Pretyman jump over the table and say: "Fall on my neck and embrace me." (Loud laughter.) Instead of that, he stiffened up, his face wreathed with anger, and he said, "The Budget is more unjust than ever." (Laughter and cheers.) Oh! no. We are placing the burdens on the broad shoulders. (Cheers.) Why should I put burdens on the people? I am one of the children of the people. (Loud and prolonged cheering, and a voice, "Bravo, David; stand by the people and they will stand by you.") I was brought up amongst them. I know their trials; and God forbid that I should add one grain of trouble to the anxiety which they bear with such patience and fortitude. (Cheers.) When the Prime Minister did me the honour of inviting me to take charge of the National Exchquer (A voice, "He knew what he was about," and laughter) at a time of great difficulty, I made up my mind, in framing the Budget which was in front of me, that at any rate no cupboard should be bared (loud cheers), no lot would be harder to bear. (Cheers.) By that test, I challenge them to judge the Budget.' (Loud and long-continued cheers, during which the right hon. gentleman resumed his seat.) Afterwards the audience rose and sang, *For he's a jolly good fellow.*

A resolution was carried in favour of the Budget.

(3b) Extract from Lord Lansdowne's speech on the Finance Bill, in the House of Lords 22 November 1909

(Parliamentary Debates, House of Lords, 1909 *vol 4 cols 731–750*)

... the case which I have to make is, after all, a very simple one. What we have to say about this Bill is this. It is a grave and I think I should be justified in saying an unprecedented measure. It has never been before the people of this country. It needs the concurrence of the House of Lords. The House of Lords should not, in our opinion, undertake the responsibility of giving that concurrence until it has become aware that the people of this country desire that this Bill should become law.

... this Bill seems to me, if I may say so, to go out of its way in ousting the Lords from their legitimate opportunities of dealing with the subject-matter of the Bill. I may remind your Lordships that in 1907 a Land Valuation Bill dealing with Scotland came before this House, and that your Lordships declined to pass it into law. The following year a similar Bill came before you again. On that occasion you amended it, your Amendments were not accepted, and the Bill was dropped. Now your Lordships will observe that on both of those occasions this question of land valuation was presented to you as a matter with which you were perfectly competent and entitled to deal, and it does seem to me to be a thing unheard of, after that has taken place, that you should now be told that because a measure of precisely the same sort is grafted on to this Finance Bill you are to be deprived of the opportunity which, by common admission, was yours in 1907 and 1908. Again in 1908 your Lordships rejected a Licensing Bill proposed by His Majesty's Government. In the case of the licensing provisions of this Bill you have an equally cynical invasion of your Lordships' rights and privileges. You have included in this Bill another Licensing Bill every bit as crushing in its severity—more crushing in its severity—than the Bill of 1908 with which you had the right to deal, and you are told that you are precluded from dealing with it because it is bound up in the cover of a Finance Bill. I ask your Lordships, what self-respecting Second Chamber would tolerate such treatment?

Oliver Cromwell invented a little House of Lords of his own for the express purpose—as he put it—of protecting the people of England against "an omnipotent House of Commons—the horridest arbitrariness that ever existed in the world". I think we detect signs of this horrid arbitrariness in the measure which we are now discussing. In all seriousness, my Lords, we have a right to ask where this kind of thing is going to stop. If you can graft Licensing Bills and Land Valuation Bills and measures of that kind on the Finance Bill, what is to prevent your grafting on it, let us say, a Home Rule Bill—setting up an authority in Ireland to collect and dispense all the taxes of that country? There is literally no limit to the abuses which might creep in if such a practice were allowed to go on without restriction. Upon this ground alone I venture to think your Lordship's House might consider very seriously whether you are justified in passing this Bill into law.

... I trust ... I have said enough to show your Lordships that the question before you is not whether you *can* reject this Bill but whether you *ought* to reject this Bill—a wholly different thing. You have to consider its results as they would affect all classes of the community, and the principles that underlie it, and you have to consider whether the people of this country have been consulted with regard to it. If you find that the results are likely to be disastrous and that the principles underlying it, which we detect not only from the official utterance of members of the Government but also from the more indiscreet explanations of so-called supporters of the Government, are pernicious and that the whole matter is one that has never been duly referred to the people of this country, then I venture to say that your Lordships have a clear duty before you—not to decree the final extinction of the Bill—because that is not what we propose, but to insist that before it becomes law an authoritative expression of the opinion of the electors of the United Kingdom shall have reached us with regard to it. ...

... We shall be asked whether we have considered the consequences of rejecting the Budget. My Lords, we have considered them, and we are ready to face them. What are those consequences? I am told in the first place that there is to be a political deadlock. You will have a Government supported by a huge majority in one House of Parliament, with a minority in the other, and that Government deprived for the moment of the control of the purse. Obviously that would constitute a deadlock. But how long need it last? You hold the key in your own hands. You tell us constantly that you desire to put these issues to the test. Why blame us if we suggest you should do it as soon as possible? Is your Budget so perishable that it will not keep for six weeks?

Then, my Lords, there is a deadlock of another kind. There is a financial deadlock which is described to us in lurid colours. Revenue will cease to come in. There will be no money to pay the troops, or to pay old-age pensions, or to pay even the salaries of His Majesty's Ministers. . . . The whole thing is to culminate in a deficit of fifty millions—I think that is the accepted figure—and in chaos, irreparable chaos. . . . Of course you can have chaos if you want to have chaos, but if you don't want to have chaos I am pretty well convinced you need not have it. . . . So far, however, as that part of the case is concerned, I for one very much prefer temporary dislocation—temporary chaos, if you like to call it so—to the permanent dislocation and permanent chaos which I honestly believe would arise out of the passage of this Bill.

There are yet other consequences which we are told to consider. We are told to think well of the consequences to this House. That is conveyed to us in various tones, sometimes full of solicitude, and sometimes minatory and violent. It is in effect intimated to us that as the penalty of rejecting this Bill we are to expect an attempt to deprive this House of its constitutional right of dealing with money Bills. . . . I am not greatly alarmed by these threats. I recall to mind that, before the Budget was dreamt of, the same threats were held over our heads. We were told long before this Budget could even have been thought of by its authors that the question of curtailment of the rights of the House of Lords was to be the dominant issue at the next election. . . . We are therefore justified in assuming that, whatever happens, this struggle has got to come. What I would venture to ask those noble Lords who may doubt whether we are wise in facing it now is this—Shall we stand better or shall we stand worse when the struggle comes if we shirk our responsibility now?

A great principle is at stake. That comes first. But, after all, even if you choose to set principle aside, what should we gain by refusing to act upon our undoubted rights in regard to this Bill? Depend upon it, my Lords, the people of this country will think worse and not better of us if we have not the courage of our

opinions, and do not, as I conceive it to be our duty to do,
appeal from you to them. . . . But I believe that the worst and
most damaging thing that you can do would be that you should
fail those who look to you as the guardians of their greatest
constitutional right, the right to be consulted when fundamental
political changes are demanded by the Government of the day;
and, my Lords, depend upon it that by rejecting this Bill you
will, on the one hand, insist that that right shall be respected;
you will not usurp the function of granting aid and supplies to
the Crown; you will not pronounce a final verdict upon this
Bill, bad though you may believe it to be; but you will say that
it is a Bill to which you have no right to give your indispensable
consent until you have been assured by the people of the country
that they desire it to pass into law.'

(3c) *Extract from* The Times, *30 November 1909*
Today will be signalised by an event of the highest constitutional
and historical importance—the exercise by the House of Lords
of an unquestionable and indispensable right which it has not
been necessary to use for a very long time, thanks to the wise
moderation with which upon the whole our Constitution has
been worked by statesmen of all parties. That traditional moderation, without which an unwritten Constitution is an impossible
contrivance has been abandoned by the present Government;
and the House of Lords has accordingly been compelled, either
to fall back upon the use of a weapon reserved for dire emergen-
cies or to submit to effacement as an efficient Second Chamber.
. . . There is no precedent for a Government avowedly pursuing
the policy of destroying the power of the House of Lords to
reject or amend any measure that a temporary majority in the
Commons may be pleased to pass, whether that measure be
desired or disliked by the country. But that, and nothing else,
has been the declared policy of the present Government, and the
Budget is merely the culmination of a design deliberately
adopted and steadily pursued.

(3d) *Extract from Mr Asquith's speech in the House of Commons,*
2 December 1909
(Parliamentary Debates, House of Commons, 1909 *5th Series vol*
13 cols 546–558)

The Prime Minister (Mr Asquith) moved, That the action of the House of Lords in refusing to pass into law the financial provision made by this House for the Service of the year is a breach of the Constitution and a usurpation of the rights of the Commons.

We are met here this afternoon under circumstances which are unexampled in the history of the British Parliament. Nearly ten months ago the Sovereign, in a paragraph in the gracious Speech from the Throne, addressed to the House of Commons, and to the House of Commons alone, invited us to make provision for the heavy additional expenditure which is due to the necessities of social reform and of national defence. In a Session which, if not for the actual length of its duration, certainly for the strenuousness of its labours, is, I believe, almost without a rival, we have addressed ourselves to that task. Never in the history of this House have more time and labour—rarely, if ever, have so much time and labour—been given to the construction and to the consideration of any proposal as were given to the Budget of this year. Never, I would add, has the process of deliberation and amendment been more free and untrammelled. Never has more consideration been given to everything that was put forward in the way either of suggestion or of criticism. When a short time ago the Finance Bill received its third reading, and as it left this House, it represented, I believe, in a greater degree than can be said of any measure of our time, the matured, and well-sifted, the deliberate work of an overwhelming majority of the representatives of the people, upon a matter which, by the custom of generations, and by the course of a practically unbroken authority, is the province of this House and of this House alone. In the course of a week, or little more than a week, the whole of this fabric has been thrown to the ground. For the first time in English history, the grant of the whole Ways and Means for the Supply and Service of the year—a grant made at the request of the Crown to the Crown by the Commons—has been intercepted and nullified by a body which admittedly has not the power to increase or to diminish one single tax, or to propose any substitute or alternative for any one of the taxes. The House of Commons would, in the judgment of His Majesty's Government, be unworthy of its past and of the traditions of which it is the custodian and the trustee if it allowed another day to pass without making it clear that it does not mean to brook the greatest indignity, and I will add the most arrogant usurpation, to which, for more than two centuries, it has been asked to submit.

*   *   *

The truth is that all this talk about the duty or the right of the House of Lords to refer measures to the people is, in the light of our practical and actual experience, the hollowest outcry of political cant. We never hear of it, as I pointed out, when a Tory Government is in power. It is never suggested when measures are thrust by a Tory majority by the aid of the guillotine and the Closure, and all the rest of it, through this House—measures which, unlike every one of the governing provisions of the Budget of the present year, have never been approved or even submitted to the electorate. It is simply a thin rhetorical veneer, by which it is sought to gloss over the partisan, and in this case the unconstitutional, action of the purely partisan Chamber. The sum and substance of the matter is that the House of Lords rejected the Finance Bill last Tuesday, not because they love the people, but because they hate the Budget. (An Hon. Member: 'And fear the brewers.') This Motion, which I am now about to propose is confined in terms to the new and unprecedented claim made by the House of Lords to interfere with finance. But I am sure, in fact I know, I am speaking the mind of my colleagues, and, I believe, of the great bulk of those who are sitting on this side of the House, when I say that it represents a stage—a momentous and, perhaps, a decisive stage—in a protracted controversy which is drawing to a close. The real question which emerges from the political struggles in this country for the last 30 years is not whether you will have a single or a double chamber system of government, but whether when the Tory Party is in power the House of Commons shall be omnipotent, and whether when the Liberal Party is in power the House of Lords shall be omnipotent.

We are living under a system of false balances and loaded dice. When the democracy votes Tory we are submitted to the uncontrolled domination of a single Chamber. When the democracy votes Liberal, a dormant Second Chamber wakes up from its slumbers and is able to frustrate and nullify our efforts, as it did with regard to education, as it did with regard to licensing, as it has done again this year with regard to measures for Scotland, and with regard to finance. I cannot exhaust the list; it would be too long. They proceed to frustrate and nullify the clearest and most plainly expressed intention of the elective House. The House of Lords have deliberately chosen their ground. They have elected to set at nought in regard to finance the unwritten and time-honoured conventions of our Constitution. In so doing, whether they foresaw it or not, they have opened out a wider and a more far-reaching issue. We have not provoked the challenge, but we welcome it. We believe that the first principles of representative government, as embodied in our slow and ordered but ever-broadening constitutional development, are at stake, and we ask the House of Commons by this Resolution to-day, as at the earliest possible moment we shall ask the constituencies of the country, to declare that the organ, the voice of the free people of this country, is to be found in the elective representatives of the nation.

4. PARLIAMENT ACT 1911

The Parliament Act was the final solution to the problems raised by the Lords' rejection of the Budget in 1909 and by the subsequent constitutional crisis. It was introduced into the Commons by the Prime Minister on 21 February 1911. Having passed the Commons, it reached the House of Lords on 23 May, and became the subject of one of the fiercest debates ever known there. The final debate in the Lords took place on 9 and 10 August. The King, George V, had let it be known that a rejection of the Bill would be followed by the creation of a large number of new peers in order to ensure that the Bill would pass when introduced again. After a very dramatic debate, in which the result was uncertain until the end, the Bill passed the House of Lords by 131 votes to 114.

The Act marks an important milestone in the evolution of the constitution. It was intended to be the prelude to a complete reform of the House of Lords, but its immediate effect was to readjust the balance between the two Houses and to put a curb on the power of the House of Lords to reject legislation passed by the Commons. The House of Lords, however, retained the power to amend and delay legislation. The Act is a short one and is given here in full.

PARLIAMENT ACT 1911

(Public General Acts 1 and 2 Geo 5 c 13)

An Act to make provision with respect to the powers of the House of Lords in relation to those of the House of Commons, and to limit the duration of Parliament. (18 August 1911)

Whereas it is expedient that provision should be made for regulating the relations between the two Houses of Parliament:

And whereas it is intended to substitute for the House of Lords as it at present exists a Second Chamber constituted on a popular instead of hereditary basis, but such substitution cannot be immediately brought into operation:

And whereas provision will require hereafter to be made by Parliament in a measure effecting such substitution for limiting and defining the powers of the new Second Chamber, but it is expedient to make such provision as in this Act appears for restricting the existing powers of the House of Lords:

Be it therefore enacted . . .

1. (1) If a Money Bill, having been passed by the House of Commons, and sent up to the House of Lords at least one month before the end of the session, is not passed by the House of Lords without amendment within one month after it is so sent up to that House, the Bill shall, unless the House of Commons direct to the contrary, be presented to His Majesty and become an Act of Parliament on the Royal Assent being signified, notwithstanding that the House of Lords have not consented to the Bill.

(2) A Money Bill means a Public Bill which in the opinion of the Speaker of the House of Commons contains only provisions dealing with all or any of the following subjects, namely, the imposition, repeal, remission, alteration, or regulation of taxation; the imposition for the payment of debt or other financial purposes of Charges on the Consolidated Fund, or on money provided by Parliament, or the variation or repeal of any such charges; supply; the appropriation, receipt, custody, issue or audit of accounts of public money; the raising or guarantee of any loan or the repayment thereof; or subordinate matters incidental to those subjects or any of them. In this subsection the expressions 'taxation,' 'public money,' and 'loan' respectively do not include any taxation, money, or loan raised by local authorities or bodies for local purposes.

(3) There shall be endorsed on every Money Bill when it is sent up to the House of Lords and when it is presented to His Majesty for assent the certificate of the Speaker of the House of Commons signed by him that it is a Money Bill. Before giving his certificate, the Speaker shall consult, if practicable, two members to be appointed from the Chairman's Panel at the beginning of each Session by the Committee of Selection.

2. (1) If any Public Bill (other than a Money Bill or a Bill containing any provision to extend the maximum duration of Parliament beyond five years) is passed by the House of Commons in three successive sessions (whether of the same Parliament or not), and, having been sent up to the House of Lords at least one month before the end of the session, is rejected by the House of Lords in each of those sessions, that Bill shall, on its rejection for the third time by the House of Lords, unless the House of Commons direct to the contrary, be presented to His

Majesty and become an Act of Parliament on the Royal Assent being signified thereto, notwithstanding that the House of Lords have not yet consented to the Bill: Provided that this provision shall not take effect unless two years have elapsed between the date of the second reading in the first of those sessions of the Bill in the House of Commons and the date on which it passes the House of Commons in the third of those sessions.

(2) When a Bill is presented to His Majesty for assent in pursuance of the provisions of this section, there shall be endorsed on the Bill the certificate of the Speaker of the House of Commons signed by him that the provisions of this section have been duly complied with.

(3) A Bill shall be deemed to be rejected by the House of Lords if it is not passed by the House of Lords either without amendment or with such amendments only as may be agreed to by both Houses.

(4) A Bill shall be deemed to be the same Bill as a former Bill sent up to the House of Lords in the preceding session if, when it is sent up to the House of Lords, it is identical with the former Bill or contains only such alterations as are certified by the Speaker of the House of Commons to be necessary owing to the time which has elapsed since the date of the former Bill, or to represent any amendments which have been made by the House of Lords in the former Bill in the preceding session, and any amendments which are certified by the Speaker to have been made by the House of Lords in the third session and agreed to by the House of Commons shall be inserted in the Bill as presented for Royal Assent in pursuance of this section:

Provided that the House of Commons may, if they think fit, on the passage of such a Bill through the House in the second or third session, suggest any further amendments without inserting the amendments in the Bill, and any such suggested amendments shall be considered by the House of Lords, and, if agreed to by that House, shall be treated as amendments made by the House of Lords and agreed to by the House of Commons; but the exercise of this power by the House of Commons shall not affect the operation of this section in the event of the Bill being rejected by the House of Lords.

3. Any certificate of the Speaker of the House of Commons given

under this Act shall be conclusive for all purposes, and shall not be questioned in any court of law.

4. (1) In every Bill presented to His Majesty under the preceding provisions of this Act, the words of enactment shall be as follows, that is to say:

'Be it enacted by the King's most Excellent Majesty, by and with the advice and consent of the Commons in this present Parliament assembled, in accordance with the provisions of the Parliament Act, 1911, and by authority of the same, as follows.'

(2) Any alteration of a Bill necessary to give effect to this section shall not be deemed to be an amendment of this Bill.

5. In this Act the expression 'Public Bill' does not include any Bill for confirming a Provisional Order.

6. Nothing in this Act shall diminish or qualify the existing rights and privileges of the House of Commons.

7. Five years shall be substituted for seven years as the time fixed for the maximum duration of Parliament under the Septennial Act, 1715.

8. This Act may be cited as the Parliament Act, 1911.

5. SOUTH AFRICA ACT 1909

In 1907, only five years after the ending of the South African War, colonial self-government was granted to the Orange Free State and the Transvaal. It paved the way for a united South Africa. In 1908 a National Convention met at Durban, consisting of representatives from each of the four South African colonies. The convention prepared a constitution for a united South Africa which, after some amendments, was accepted by the four colonies, and was passed by the British Parliament as the South Africa Act 1909. The new constitution came into force in 1910. Lord Gladstone became the first Governor-General of the Union and General Botha, the former Boer leader, was the first Prime Minister. The act is long and detailed, setting out the Constitution of the Union of South Africa and of the provinces. The following extracts contain some of its main provisions.

SOUTH AFRICA ACT 1909

(Public General Acts 9 Ed c 9)

An Act to constitute the Union of South Africa. (20 September 1909)

Whereas it is desirable for the welfare and future progress of South Africa that the several British Colonies therein should be united under one Government in a legislative union under the Crown of Great Britain and Ireland:

And whereas it is expedient to make provision for the union of the Colonies of the Cape of Good Hope, Natal, the Transvaal, and the Orange River Colony on terms and conditions to which they have agreed by resolution of their respective Parliaments, and to define the executive, legislative, and judicial powers to be exercised in the government of the Union:

And whereas it is expedient to make provision for the establishment of provinces with the powers of legislation and administration in local matters and in such other matters as may be specially reserved for provincial legislation and administration:

And whereas it is expedient to provide for the eventual admission into the Union or transfer to the Union of such parts of South Africa as are not originally included therein:

Be it therefore enacted . . .

The Union

4. It shall be lawful for the King, with the advice of the Privy Council, to declare by proclamation that, on and after a day therein appointed, not being later than one year after the passing of this Act, the Colonies of the Cape of Good Hope, Natal, the Transvaal, and the Orange River Colony, hereinafter called the Colonies, shall be united in a Legislative Union under one Government under the name of the Union of South Africa. On and after the day appointed by such proclamation the Government and Parliament of the Union shall have full power and authority within the limits of the Colonies, but the King may at any time after the proclamation appoint a governor-general for the Union.

* * *

6. The Colonies mentioned in section four shall become original provinces of the Union under the names of Cape of Good Hope, Natal, Transvaal, and Orange Free State, as the case may be. The original provinces shall have the same limits as the respective Colonies at the establishment of the Union.

PART III

Executive Government

8. The Executive Government of the Union is vested in the King, and shall be administered by His Majesty in person or by a governor-general as His representative.

9. The Governor-General shall be appointed by the King, and shall have and may exercise in the Union during the King's pleasure, but subject to this Act, such power and functions of the King as His Majesty may be pleased to assign to him.

10. There shall be payable to the King out of the Consolidated Revenue Fund of the Union for the salary of the Governor-General an annual sum of ten thousand pounds. The salary of the Governor-General shall not be altered during his continuance in office.

* * *

12. There shall be an Executive Council to advise the Governor-General in the government of the Union, and the members of the council shall be chosen and summoned by the Governor-General and sworn as executive councillors, and shall hold office during his pleasure.

* * *

14. The Governor-General may appoint officers not exceeding ten in number to administer such departments of State of the Union as the Governor-General in Council may establish; such officers shall hold office during the pleasure of the Governor-General. They shall be members of the Executive Council and shall be the King's ministers of State for the Union. After the first general election of members of the House of Assembly, as hereinafter provided, no minister shall hold office for a longer period than three months unless he is or becomes a member of either House of Parliament.

* * *

17. The command in chief of the naval and military forces within the Union is vested in the King or in the Governor-General as his representative.

18. Save as in section twenty-three excepted, Pretoria shall be the seat of Government of the Union.

PART IV

Parliament

19. The legislative power of the Union shall be vested in the Parliament of the Union, herein called Parliament, which shall consist of the King, a Senate, and a House of Assembly.

20. The Governor-General may appoint such times for holding the sessions of Parliament as he thinks fit and may also from time to time, by proclamation or otherwise, prorogue Parliament, and may in like manner dissolve the Senate and the House of Assembly simultaneously, or the House of Assembly alone: provided that the Senate shall not be dissolved within a period of ten years after the establishment of the Union, and provided further that the dissolution of the Senate shall not affect any senators nominated by the Governor-General in Council.

21. Parliament shall be summoned to meet not later than six months after the establishment of the Union.

22. There shall be a session of Parliament once at least in every year, so that a period of twelve months shall not intervene between the last sitting of Parliament in one session and its first sitting in the next session.

23. Cape Town shall be the seat of the Legislature of the Union.

Senate

24. For ten years after the establishment of the Union the constitution of the Senate shall, in respect of the original provinces, be as follows:

(i) Eight senators shall be nominated by the Governor-General in Council, and for each original province eight senators shall be elected in the manner hereinafter provided.

(ii) The senators to be nominated by the Governor-General in Council shall hold their seats for ten years. One half of their number shall be selected on the ground mainly of their thorough experience or otherwise, with the reasonable wants and wishes of the coloured races in South Africa. If the seat of a senator so nominated shall become vacant, the Governor-General in Council shall nominate another person to be a senator, who shall hold his seat for ten years.

(iii) After the passing of this Act and before the day appointed for the establishment of the Union, the Governor of each of the Colonies shall summon a special sitting of both Houses of the Legislature, and the two Houses sitting together as one body and presided over by the Speaker of the Legislative Assembly shall elect eight persons to be senators for the province. Such senators shall hold their seats for ten years. If the seat of a senator so elected shall become vacant, the provincial council of the province for which such senator has been elected shall choose a person to hold the seat until the completion of the period for which the person in whose stead he is elected would have held his seat.

25. Parliament may provide for the manner in which the Senate shall be constituted after the expiration of ten years. . . .

26. The qualifications of a senator shall be as follows: He must—

(a) be not less than thirty years of age;

(b) be qualified to be registered as a voter for the election of members of the House of Assembly in one of the provinces;

(c) have resided for five years within the limits of the Union as existing at the time when he is elected or nominated, as the case may be;

(d) be a British subject of European descent;

(e) in the case of an elected senator, be the registered owner of immovable property within the Union of the value of not less than five hundred pounds over and above any special mortgages thereon.

For the purpose of this section, residence in, and property situated within, a colony before its incorporation in the Union shall be treated as residence in and property situated within the Union.

*   *   *

House of Assembly

32. The House of Assembly shall be composed of members directly chosen by the voters of the Union in electoral divisions delimited as hereinafter provided.

33. The number of members to be elected in the original provinces at the first election and until the number is altered in accordance with the provisions of this Act shall be as follows:

Cape of Good Hope	Fifty-one
Natal	Seventeen
Transvaal	Thirty-six
Orange Free State	Seventeen

*   *   *

35. (1) Parliament may by law prescribe the qualifications which shall be necessary to entitle persons to vote at the election of members of the House of Assembly, but no such law shall disqualify any person in the province of the Cape of Good Hope who, under the laws existing in the Colony of the Cape of Good Hope at the establishment of the Union, is or may become capable of being registered as a voter from being so registered in the province of the Cape of Good Hope by reason of his race or colour only, unless the Bill be passed by both Houses of Parliament sitting together, and at the third reading be agreed to by not less than two-thirds of the total number of members of both Houses. A Bill so passed at such joint sitting shall be taken to have been duly passed by both Houses of Parliament.

(2) No person who at the passing of any such law is registered as a voter in any province shall be removed from the register by reason only of any disqualification based on race or colour.

*   *   *

44. The qualifications of a member of the House of Assembly shall be as follows:

He must—
    (a) be qualified to be registered as a voter for the election of members of the House of Assembly in one of the provinces;
    (b) have resided for five years within the limits of the Union as existing at the time when he is elected.
    (c) be a British subject of European descent.

For the purposes of this section, residence in a colony before its incorporation in the Union shall be treated as residence in the Union

45. Every House of Assembly shall continue for five years from the first meeting thereof, and no longer, but may be sooner dissolved by the Governor-General.

*   *   *

Both Houses of Parliament

51. Every senator and every member of the House of Assembly shall, before taking his seat, make and subscribe before the Governor-General, or some person authorised by him, an oath or affirmation of allegiance in the following form:

Oath

I, A.B., do swear that I will be faithful and bear true allegiance to his Majesty (here insert the name of the King or Queen of the United Kingdom of Great Britain and Ireland for the time being) His (or Her) heirs and successors according to law. So help me God.

Affirmation

I, A.B., do solemnly and sincerely affirm and declare that I will be faithful and bear true allegiance to his Majesty (here insert the name of the King or Queen of the United Kingdom of Great Britain and Ireland for the time being) His (or Her) heirs and successors according to law.

*   *   *

56. Each senator and each member of the House of Assembly shall, under such rules as shall be framed by Parliament, receive an allowance of four hundred pounds a year. . . .

*   *   *

Powers of Parliament

59. Parliament shall have full power to make laws for the peace, order, and good government of the Union. . . .

PART V

The Provinces Administrators

68.   (1) In each province there shall be a chief executive officer appointed by the Governor-General in Council, who shall be styled the administrator of the province, and in whose name all executive acts relating to provincial affairs therein shall be done. . . .

*   *   *

Provincial Councils

70.   (1) There shall be a provincial council in each province consisting of the same number of members as are elected in the province for the House of Assembly: Provided that, in any province whose representatives in the House of Assembly shall be less than twenty-five in number, the provincial council shall consist of twenty-five members.

(2) Any person qualified to vote for the election of members of the provincial council shall be qualified to be a member of such council.

*   *   *

77. There shall be freedom of speech in the provincial council, and no member shall be liable to any action or proceeding in any court by reason of his speech or vote in such council.

*   *   *

Powers of Provincial Councils

85. Subject to the provisions of the Act and the assent of the Governor-General in Council as hereinafter provided, the provincial council may make ordinances in relation to matters coming within the following classes of subjects (that is to say):

(i) Direct taxation within the province in order to raise a revenue for provincial purposes;

(ii) The borrowing of money on the sole credit of the province with the consent of the Governor-General in Council and in accordance with regulations to be framed by Parliament;

(iii) Education, other than higher education, for a period of five years and hereafter until Parliament otherwise provides:

(iv) Agriculture to the extent and subject to the conditions to be defined by Parliament:

(v) The establishment, maintenance and management of hospitals and charitable institutions:

(vi) Municipal institutions, divisional councils, and other local institutions of a similar nature:

(vii) Local works and undertakings within the province, other than railways and harbours and other than such works as extend beyond the borders of the province, and subject to the power of Parliament to declare any work a national work and to provide for its construction by arrangement with the provincial council or otherwise:

(viii) Roads, outspans, ponts, and bridges, other than bridges connecting two provinces:

(ix) Markets and pounds:

(x) Fish and game preservation:

(xi) The imposition of punishment by fine, penalty, or imprisonment for enforcing any law or any ordinance of the province made in relation to any matter coming within any of the classes of subjects enumerated in this section:

(xii) Generally all matters which, in the opinion of the Governor-General in Council, are of a merely local or private nature in the province:

(xiii) All other subjects in respect of which Parliament shall by any law delegate the power of making ordinances to the provincial council.

* * *

Miscellaneous

94. The seats of provincial government shall be:

For the Cape of Good Hope	Cape Town
For Natal	Pietermaritzburg
For the Transvaal	Pretoria
For the Orange Free State	Bloemfontein

PART VI

The Supreme Court of South Africa

95. There shall be a Supreme Court of South Africa consisting of a Chief Justice of South Africa, the ordinary judges of appeal, and the other judges of the several divisions of the Supreme Court of South Africa in the provinces.

* * *

PART VIII

General

137. Both the English and Dutch languages shall be official languages of the Union, and shall be treated on a footing of equality, and possess and enjoy equal freedom, rights, and privileges; all records, journals, and proceedings of Parliament shall be kept in both languages, and all Bills, Acts, and notices of general public importance or interest issued by the Government of the Union shall be in both languages.

*   *   *

145. The services of officers in the public service of any of the Colonies at the establishment of the Union shall not be dispensed with by reason of their want of knowledge of either the English or Dutch language.

*   *   *

147. The control and administration of native affairs and of matters specially or differentially affecting Asiatics throughout the Union shall vest in the Governor-General in Council. . . .

6. PAYMENT OF
MEMBERS OF PARLIAMENT 1911

The demand that members of the House of Commons should receive salaries had been made during the nineteenth century, notably by the Chartists, and it had been part of the policy of the Liberal Party for several years, though it had not been given very much prominence. The main reason why it came to the forefront in 1911 was because of the difficult situation created by the Osborne Judgment. In 1908 a railwayman, W. V. Osborne, was successful in obtaining a judgment preventing Trade Unions from providing for parliamentary representation by means of a compulsory levy on members. This judgment caused considerable hardship to many Labour members of Parliament, who had been supported from Trade Union funds, and on 10 August 1911, the day on which the Parliament Bill was passed by the House of Lords, Lloyd George introduced the motion that members should be paid a salary of £400 a year. This motion was passed by the House of Commons by 256 votes to 158. Extracts are given below from the speech of Lloyd George and from the speech of Arthur Lee, who was one of the principal opposition speakers. An extract is also given from *The Times* leading article on the subject.

(6a) *Extract from* The Times *10 August 1911*

The Chancellor of the Exchequer is to move today a resolution declaring that in the opinion of the House of Commons provision should be made for paying £400 a year to every member of the House except Ministers, officers of the House, and officers of the King's Household. . . . Payment of members is a large question of policy. It will hardly be questioned by any one on either side of the House that the innovation must have far-reaching effects upon our representative system, and upon the composition and quality of the House of Commons. There are probably very few upon either side who, if free to express their real opinions, would not hold that the effects of the change must be highly undesirable. The House of Commons does not want payment of members and, if a Bill were introduced and freely debated, there can be no doubt that the proposal would call forth some severe criticism from the Government's own supporters. A method is, therefore, chosen which as far as possible eliminates examination of the question, and coerces the party into treating it simply as one of confidence in the Government. A Supplementary Estimate is brought in for £252,000. It is part of the Budgetary provision for the year and therefore not to be lightly meddled with by any supporter of the Government. When the resolution is passed by a purely party vote under the manipulation of the Whips the payment will be included in the Appropriation Bill, and the trick will be played. A thing which the country does not want, and which the House of Commons does not want, will be done simply because it is convenient for the oligarchs of the front bench to do it in order to escape, or try to escape, from a temporary difficulty.

This is an example of the oligarchic tyranny to be practised under the Single Chamber government to which we are now virtually reduced. . . . There is no mandate and no desire for the proposed change among the members of the House of Commons. There is not even so much as conviction or belief among members of the Government that payment of members will be good for the country. Some such belief will very probably be feigned today, but it will not impose upon anyone. It is perfectly well known to all the world that the Government have no conviction or belief of the kind, and that payment of members would never have been proposed by them were it not that they do not know how to meet the difficulty of dealing with the Osborne judgment. They have merely snatched at payment of members as an expedient for getting round that inconvenience. They know well enough that their expedient must have permanent and far-reaching consequences which, so far as human foresight can go, will be evil. That does not matter in the least, or rather it matters only to the extent that they proceed to rush the matter through without giving either the House or the country time to consider what the consequences will be. If anything could add to the cynicism of their proceedings, it is supplied by the fact that they have not so much as the assurance that payment of members will secure the object they have in view. The whole thing is merely a gambler's throw. The Labour Party are quite ready to take the payment, but they have made it plain that they do not on that account relinquish their demand for what they call the reversal of the Osborne judgment. All that the Government have to go upon is a speculation.

They hope that in some way the payment of members will put them in a better position as against the Labour Party, should that party persist, as it has declared it will persist, in pressing its demand. That is the miserable mess of pottage for which the Government are ready to sacrifice the permanent interests of the nation.

(*6b*) *Extracts from the speeches of Lloyd George and Arthur Lee in the House of Commons 10 August 1911*
(Parliamentary Debates, House of Commons, *5th Series vol 29 cols 1365–1393*)

The Chancellor of the Exchequer (Mr Lloyd George):

I rise to move the important Motion that stands in my name:

'That, in the opinion of this House, provision should be made for the payment of a salary at the rate of four hundred pounds a year to every Member of this House, excluding any Member who is for the time being in receipt of a salary as an officer of the House, or as a Minister, or as an officer of His Majesty's Household.' . . .

This is the only Parliament in the world where no contribution at all is made towards the expenses incurred by any Member in the discharge of his duty, and it is only in comparatively recent times that this Parliament has been in that position. It is true that there are Parliaments where no payment is made by way of salary. In those cases there are certain contributions towards expenses. That is the case in Spain and in Italy. But taking every other great Parliament in the world there is a payment made to members of so much towards the cost of maintenance. It is said that in proposing this we are departing from some great British tradition. As a matter of fact, we are reverting to an old British tradition. The old tradition of this House was that Members were paid. (An hon. Member: 'By the constituencies.') They will be paid still by the constituencies. The only difference is that instead of being a charge on the rates, which I am sure hon. Members opposite would deprecate, it is a charge on the Imperial taxes. . . .

. . . The work of Parliament is greater, infinitely greater; it is greater in the quantity and volume of work. Not only that, but it is very much greater in the attention it demands at the hands of each individual Member. In the old days, how was the work of Parliament really done? Anybody who cares to look at Hansard, the old Hansard, will find that the work of Parliament was practically in the hands of very few Members. Anybody who conducts a Bill through this House knows that that is not the case any longer. On the contrary, every Member of Parliament not merely has the right to intervene in Debate, but exercises that right frequently. . . .

. . . If hon. Members will take the trouble to look not merely at Hansard, but at the old Division lists, they will find that although there was practically the same number of Members in this House as we have got now, the attendance was by no means general. The bulk of Members were absent during the greater part of the Session. The Divisions were small; there would be a great whip up for a big Division on a big Bill. What happened to Members in the meantime? They were down in the country, in their country houses, or those who attended to business were down attending to business. There was nothing then to prevent a Member of Parliament being a loyal member of his party and giving all the support which a Government values most. I think I will not dwell upon that. I think it will be thoroughly appreciated. They came up when they were really needed, and they were conveniently absent when it was necessary to get on with business. . . .

. . . In the old days we had practically only two classes here. We had the great county families and the legal profession, and we had odds and ends coming in; but, in the main, representation was confined to these two great classes. Since then you have brought in one class after another—the great middle class—the labouring population, and factory representation. I think everybody will agree that this process of broadening has raised the average of the House. . . .

. . . What is the demand embodied in this Resolution? It is practically a demand from a democracy, which still is under the impression, and, I think, sound impression, that it is labouring under a good many ills that Parliament alone can remedy. . . .

Instead of confining, as it were, those who were able to remedy their evils and cure them to a small class, they say, 'We want an unlimited choice in picking out the men who will suit us best.' . . .

. . . After the Osborne Judgment we are left face to face with this proposition. We must either be restricted to a limited choice, which we have got at the present moment, or find some method whereby men of limited means, who have a capacity as well as a desire for public service, should be able to come to this House. . . . There is a large and growing class whose presence in this House, in my judgment, is highly desirable, men of wide culture, of high intelligence, and of earnest purpose, whose services in this House would be invaluable in the interests of the community as a whole, who I think would lift the level of discussion, and who would contribute to it in every respect, but whose limited means prevent their taking up a political career. That class of man is very largely excluded at the present moment unless he makes large sacrifices, which it is impossible for him to make, if he has a wife and family. Such a man, with £400 a year to fall back upon, could take his chance of earning the rest in such times as he could devote to his professional or other business. . . .

. . . When we offer £400 a year as payment of Members of Parliament it is not a recognition of the magnitude of the service, it is not a remuneration, it is not a recompense, it is not even a salary. It is just an allowance, and I think the minimum allowance, to enable men to come here, men who would render incalculable service to the State, and whom it is an incalculable loss to the State not to have here, but who cannot be here because their means do not allow it.

*　　*　　*

(6c) *Arthur Lee:*

. . . We feel very seriously upon this subject, and we have endeavoured—I have endeavoured, I may say, after consultation with my hon. Friends who sit on this side and with their approval—to express briefly the grounds upon which we object to this Motion in the Amendment . . . which is in these words:

'To leave out from the word "that" to the end, and to add the words: "this House declines to provide money for the payment of Members of Parliament, because such payment would be an indefensible violation of the principle of gratuitous public service, would involve the taxpayers in heavy and unnecessary expense, and would encourage a demand on the part of members of local bodies to be paid for their services, and further because, in the opinion of this House, there would be a peculiar impropriety in Members of Parliament voting salaries to themselves".' . . .

In my personal belief the effect of this change upon the public life of this country will be even more marked and even more disastrous than the passage of the Parliament Bill itself. . . . What could be more significant of the evils of Single-Chamber Government which we are now faced with in the immediate future than the attitude of the Government and the House of Commons towards this great question ? . . . On Tuesday of this week the House of Commons finally parted with the Parliament Bill, which confers upon it complete financial control. And here on Thursday of the same week . . . the Members of the House of Commons . . . are proceeding without more ado, without even observing the ordinary decencies of Parliamentary procedure, to confer this benefit upon themselves. . . . I contend that the Government cannot in any shape or form claim that they have a mandate, and I entirely deny that the country has given any sanction, either explicitly or tacitly, to the proposal the Government have now brought forward. But if the proceeding of the Government is irregular and open to legitimate suspicion, in our view the principle contained in the Resolution is both objectionable and unnecessary. I go further and say that the Government's policy in this matter is futile, because it was almost admitted today, and it has been frequently said, at any rate in the past, that one of the main objects of the payment of Members was to meet the grievance of the Labour Party in regard to the Osborne Judgment. That was the excuse made, and there is hardly use concealing the fact that the measure was brought in —there are many Members who are behind the Government who do not like it—frankly to square the Labour party in connection with the Osborne Judgment. The Labour Party deny that it is a remedy, and they have not accepted it as such. . . . The real fact, of course, is this, that whatever be the amount of the salary which the Government propose, it will not meet the real grievances of the Labour Party in regard to the Osborne Judgment. It does not give them what they are really after, and that is, the political control of the trade union funds. . . . In my view the disadvantages of this proposal are both cumulative and overwhelming. In the first place I think this proposal must lead to the loss of the moral authority of the House of Commons in the public mind, and if we are to have the House of Commons established as a Single Chamber with the control of the destinies of the country in its hands there is one thing it needs more than anything else, and that is moral authority. I also object to Members of Parliament in future becoming the mere paid delegates of their constituency rather than their free and independent representatives, because I believe it will lead to the extinction of that type of Member in the House of Commons who has been its peculiar pride and strength up to the present time. It will lead to the extinction of the class of Member who is active and distinguished in other walks of life, and who, in spite of having other work, does as a matter of fact attend to the business of this House because he believes it an honour and a duty to do so, but who in future will have neither time nor inclination to compete with the vast number of candidates that will come forward when the reward is not merely election to the House of Commons, but a competence—I will not say more than that—which will be paid for his work as a Member of Parliament.

This proposal has been defended by the Chancellor of the Exchequer on the ground that it is merely what he calls an allowance to make up for extra expenses. We all know that other countries started with the same modest idea. We had an official return laid on the Table of the House very recently, and if hon. Members would study what has happened in other countries they will find that they all made very small beginnings. In the United States of America they began with £180 a year, and then by successive instalments Congress raised the amount to the equivalent of £2,000 a year. In France they started with £360 a year, and it has now been increased to £600; and in addition, there are pensions for ex-members, for their widows, and for their children until they reach the age of twenty-one. In Australia there was an increase the other day in the payment of members from £400 to £600 a year, and it is absolutely inevitable that once salaries are paid to Members of Parliament who have control over the amount of their salaries, like all other classes who are paid wages, they will seek to raise those wages whenever they get the opportunity. . . .

Above all, I object to it because it will sound the death-knell of that system of voluntary service which has been the chief and unique glory of British public life . . . I have, in the eleven years I have been in this House, seen many regrettable incidents, but I cannot recall any more repellent or humiliating spectacle than the House of Commons, the very day after it has taken into its own hands by force supreme and exclusive control over the nation's finances hungrily seizing without even a decent interval, upon the first opportunity after the Bill is passed to help themselves out of the pockets of the taxpayers. The Government in this matter appears to be insatiable. Not content in this week with dragging the Crown through the mire of party politics, not content with destroying the legislative authority of the other House of Parliament, they are now proposing to destroy the moral authority of the House of Commons as well. It is because I love the House of Commons and am proud of it that I wish the votes of my hon. Friends on this side to save it, if possible, from this wanton and unnecessary humiliation.

The First World War

7. GREAT BRITAIN AND THE EUROPEAN POWERS 1914

Germany declared war against Russia on 2 August 1914 and against France on 3 August. This presented Great Britain with a difficult and dangerous situation. The issues were laid before the House of Commons by Sir Edward Grey in his speech of 3 August. The two most pressing problems were, first, whether Britain should remain neutral, and thus perhaps allow the German fleet to pass through the Straits of Dover and attack the French coast and, second, whether Britain should fulfil her treaty obligation to protect the neutrality of Belgium. Sir Edward Grey's opinion was that Britain could not remain neutral in the coming war, and his forceful presentation of his views gained support on all sides of the House. His whole speech, and in particular his emphasis upon Britain's duty to defend Belgian neutrality, made a great impression, and did much to rally opinion both within and outside Parliament behind the Government.

On the morning of 4 August German troops invaded Belgium and Asquith announced to the Commons that an ultimatum had been sent to Germany. No reply was made by the German Government to this ultimatum and at 11 p.m. (midnight in Berlin) the time limit expired and Great Britain was at war with Germany.

(*7a*) *An Extract from the Statement by the Secretary of State for Foreign Affairs (Sir Edward Grey) to the House of Commons 3 August 1914*

(Parliamentary Debates, House of Commons, 1914 *5th Series vol. 65 cols 1809 f*)

Last week I stated that we were working for peace not only for this country, but to preserve the peace of Europe. Today events move so rapidly that it is exceedingly difficult to state with technical accuracy the actual state of affairs, but it is clear that the peace of Europe cannot be preserved. Russia and Germany, at any rate, have declared war upon each other. . . .

The present crisis has originated . . . in a dispute between Austria and Servia. I can say this with the most absolute confidence—no Government and no country has less desire to be involved in war over a dispute with Austria and Servia than the Government and the country of France. They are involved in it because of their obligation of honour under a definite alliance with Russia. Well, it is only fair to say to the House that that obligation of honour cannot apply in the same way to us. We are not parties to the Franco-Russian Alliance. We do not even know the terms of that Alliance. . . . I now come to what we think the situation requires of us. For many years we have had a long-standing friendship with France. . . . But how far that friendship entails obligation . . . let every man look into his own heart, and his own feelings, and construe the extent of the obligation for himself. . . . The French fleet is now in the Mediterranean, and the Northern and Western coasts of France are absolutely undefended. The French fleet being concentrated in the Mediterranean the situation is very different from what it used to be, because the friendship which has grown up between the two countries has given them a sense of security that there was nothing to be feared from us. . . . My own feeling is that if a foreign fleet engaged in a war which France had not sought, and in which she had not been the aggressor, came down the English Channel and bombarded and battered the undefended coasts of France, we could not stand aside.

. . . We feel strongly that France was entitled to know—and to know at once!—whether or not in the event of attack upon her unprotected Northern and Western Coasts she could depend upon British support. In that emergency, and in these compelling circumstances, yesterday afternoon I gave to the French Ambassador the following statement:

'I am authorised to give an assurance that if the German Fleet comes into the Channel or through the North Sea to undertake hostile operations against the French coasts or shipping the British Fleet will give all the protection in its power....'

. . . And, Sir, there is the more serious consideration—becoming more serious every hour—there is the question of the neutrality of Belgium. . . . I will read to the House what took place last week on this subject. When mobilisation was beginning, I knew that this question must be a most important element in our policy—a most important subject for the House of Commons. I telegraphed at the same time in similar terms to both Paris and Berlin to say that it was essential for us to know whether the French and German Governments respectively were prepared to undertake an engagement to respect the neutrality of Belgium. These are the replies. I got from the French Government this reply:

'The French Government are resolved to respect the neutrality of Belgium, and it would only be in the event of some other Power violating that neutrality that France might find herself under the necessity, in order to assure the defence of her security, to act otherwise. This assurance has been given several times. The President of the Republic spoke of it to the King of the Belgians, and the French Minister at Brussels has spontaneously renewed the assurance to the Belgian Minister of Foreign Affairs today.'

From the German Government the reply was:

'The Secretary of State for Foreign Affairs could not possibly give an answer before consulting the Emperor and the Imperial Chancellor.'

Sir Edward Goschen, to whom I had said it was important to have an answer soon, said he hoped the answer would not be too long delayed. The German Minister for Foreign Affairs then gave Sir Edward Goschen to understand that he rather doubted whether they could answer at all, as any reply they might give could not fail, in the event of war, to have the undesirable effect of disclosing, to a certain extent, part of their plan of campaign.
. . .

There is but one way in which the Goverment could make certain at the present moment of keeping outside this war, and that would be that it should immediately issue a proclamation of unconditional neutrality. We cannot do that. We have made the commitment to France that I have read to the House which prevents us from doing that. We have got the consideration of

Belgium which prevents us also from any unconditional neutrality, and without those conditions absolutely satisfied and satisfactory, we are bound not to shrink from proceeding to the use of all the forces in our power. If we did take that line by saying, 'We will have nothing whatever to do with this matter' under no conditions—the Belgian Treaty obligations, the possible position in the Mediterranean, with damage to British interests, and what may happen to France from our failure to support France—if we were to say that all those things mattered nothing, were as nothing, and to say we would stand aside, we should, I believe, sacrifice our respect and good name and reputation before the world, and should not escape the most serious and grave economic consequences. . . .

(7b) The Prime Minister's Announcement to the House of Commons 4 August 1914
(Parliamentary Debates, House of Commons, 1914 5th Series vol 65 cols 1925–1927)

In conformity with the statement of policy made here by my right hon. Friend the Foreign Secretary yesterday, a telegram was early this morning sent by him to our Ambassador in Berlin. It was to this effect:

'The King of the Belgians has made an appeal to His Majesty the King for diplomatic intervention on behalf of Belgium. His Majesty's Government are also informed that the German Government has delivered to the Belgian Government a Note proposing friendly neutrality entailing free passage through Belgian territory and promising to maintain the independence and integrity of the Kingdom and its possession, at the conclusion of peace, threatening in case of refusal to treat Belgium as an enemy. An answer was requested within twelve hours. We also understand that Belgium has categorically refused this as a flagrant violation of the law of nations. His Majesty's Government are bound to protest against this violation of a Treaty to which Germany is a party in common with themselves, and must request an assurance that the demand made upon Belgium may not be proceeded with, and that her neutrality will be respected by Germany. You should ask for an immediate reply.'

We received this morning from our Minister at Brussels the following telegram:

'German Minister has this morning addressed Note to the Belgian Minister for Foreign Affairs stating that as Belgian Government have declined the well-intended proposals submitted to them by the Imperial Government, the latter will, deeply to their regret, be compelled to carry out, if necessary by force of arms, the measures considered indispensable in view of the French menaces.'

Simultaneously—almost immediately afterwards—we received from the Belgian Legation here in London the following telegram:

'General staff announces that territory has been violated at Gemmenich (near Aix-la-Chappelle).'

Subsequent information tended to show that the German force has penetrated still further into Belgian territory. We also received this morning from the German Ambassador here the telegram sent to him by the German Foreign Secretary, and communicated by the Ambassador to us. It is in these terms:

'Please dispel any mistrust that may subsist on the part of the British Government with regard to our intentions by repeating most positively formal assurance that, even in the case of armed conflict with Belgium, Germany will, under no pretence whatever, annex Belgian territory. Sincerity of this declaration is borne out by fact that we solemnly pledged our word to Holland strictly to respect her neutrality. It is obvious that we could not profitably annex Belgic territory without making, at the same time, territorial acquisitions at expense of Holland. Please impress upon Sir E. Grey that German Army could not be exposed to French attack across Belgium, which was planned according to absolutely unimpeachable information. Germany had consequently to disregard Belgic neutrality, it being for her a question of life or death to prevent French advance.'

I have to add this on behalf of His Majesty's Government: We cannot regard this as in any sense a satisfactory communication. We have, in reply to it, repeated the request we made last week to the German Government, that they should give us the same assurance in regard to Belgian neutrality as was given to us and to Belgium by France last week. We have asked that a reply to that request, and a satisfactory answer to the telegram of this morning—which I have read to the House—should be given before midnight.

8. THE DEBATE OVER STRATEGY

By November 1914 the War on the Western Front had reached a deadlock. Neither side could break through the line of enemy trenches and fortifications. This situation gave rise to the controversy between those who believed that some way round the deadlock should be sought, and that Germany and her allies should be attacked on some other front, and those who believed that the war could only be won by the defeat of the German armies on the Western Front. This controversy was to continue throughout the war. Moreover, as the months passed and as the dreadful toll of casualties mounted, many people began to feel that a crushing defeat of Germany was not possible and that some compromise solution should be sought. The following documents illustrate some of the arguments which were used.

The two men who were most active in pressing the idea of breaking the deadlock on the Western Front by an attack in some other region were Churchill and Lloyd George. Churchill, who was First Lord of the Admiralty, at first supported the plan of a combined naval and military attack upon Schleswig-Holstein. This idea was strongly favoured by Fisher, the First Sea Lord. The plan was outlined by Churchill in his letter to Asquith of 29 December 1914.

Alternative plans were put forward by Lloyd George in his Memorandum of 1 January 1915. The suggestion of an attack on Turkey soon gained the support of Churchill and of a number of other prominent members of the Government. The plan developed into the ill-fated offensive in Gallipoli during 1915.

(*8a*) *From a letter to the Prime Minister written by Winston Churchill, First Lord of the Admiralty, on 29 December 1914*
(*W. S. Churchill*—The World Crisis 1915, *pp 44–45*, *Thornton Butterworth, London 1923*)

. . . I think it quite possible that neither side will have the strength to penetrate the other's lines in the Western theatre. Belgium particularly, which it is vital to Germany to hold as a peace-counter, has no doubt been made into a mere succession of fortified lines. I think it probable that the Germans hold back several large mobile reserves of their best troops. Without attempting to take a final view, my impression is that the position of both armies is not likely to undergo any decisive change—although no doubt several hundred thousand men will be spent to satisfy the military mind on the point.

For somewhat different reasons, a similar stalemate seems likely to be reached in the Eastern theatre. When the Russians come into contact with the German railway system, they are heavily thrown back. On the other hand, withdrawn into their own country they can hold their own.

On the assumption that these views are correct, the question arises, how ought we to apply our growing military power? Are there not other alternatives than sending our armies to chew barbed wire in Flanders? Further, cannot the power of the Navy be brought more directly to bear upon the enemy? If it is impossible or unduly costly to pierce the German lines on existing fronts, ought we not, as new forces come to hand, to engage him on new frontiers, and enable the Russians to do so too? The invasion of Schleswig-Holstein from the sea would at once threaten the Kiel canal and enable Denmark to join us. The accession of Denmark would throw open the Baltic. British naval command of the Baltic would enable the Russian armies to be landed within 90 miles of Berlin; and the enemy, while being closely held on all existing lines, would be forced to face new attacks directed at vital points and exhaust himself along a still larger perimeter.

The essential preliminary is the blocking of the Heligoland debouch. The capture of a German Island for an overseas base is the first indispensable step to all these possibilities. It alone can guarantee Great Britain from raid or invasion. It enables the power of our flotillas to be applied. Its retention by us would be intolerable to the enemy, and would in all probability bring about the sea battle. . . . If (the island of) Borkum were seized, it could be held without compromising the action of the Grand Fleet. If Borkum were held, it seems to me probable that a series of events would follow leading in a few weeks to German ships being driven altogether from the North Sea and into their harbours and mined and blocked therein.

There are three phases of the naval war: first, the clearance of the seas and the recall of the foreign squadrons—that is nearly completed; second, the closing of the Elbe—that we have now to do, and third, the domination of the Baltic—that would be decisive. . . . The action of the Allies proceeds almost independently. Plans could be made now for April and May which would offer good prospects of bringing the war to its decisive stage by land and sea. We ought not to drift. We ought now to consider while time remains the scope and character we wish to impart to the war in the early summer. We ought to concert our action with our allies, and particularly with Russia. We ought to form a scheme for a continuous and progressive offensive, and be ready with the new alternative when and if the direct frontal attacks in France on the German lines and Belgium have failed, as fail I fear they will. Without your direct guidance and initiative, none of these things will be done; and a succession of bloody checks in the West and in the East will leave the Allies dashed in spirit and bankrupt in policy.

(*8b*) *From a Memorandum on War Strategy written by Lloyd George, Minister of Munitions, and circulated to the Members of the War Council, 1 January 1915*
(*D. Lloyd George*—War Memoirs, *vol I pp 369 f, Nicholson and Watson, London 1933–1936*)

Now that the new armies are in course of training and will, with the Territorials, be ready by the end of March to the extent of at least half a million men, I suggest that it is time the Government should take counsel with the military experts as to the use which shall be made of this magnificent force. It is a force of a totally different character from any which has hitherto left these shores. It has been drawn almost exclusively from the better class of artisan, the upper and the lower middle classes. In intelligence, education and character it is vastly superior to any army ever raised in this country, and as it has been drawn not from the ranks of those who have generally cut themselves off from home ties and about whose fate there is therefore not the same anxiety at home, the people of this country will take an intimate personal interest in its fate of a kind which they have never displayed before in our military expeditions. So that if this superb army is thrown away upon futile enterprises such as those we have witnessed during the last few weeks, the country will be uncontrollably indignant at the lack of provision and intelligence shown in our plans. I may add that operations such as those we have witnessed during the past few months will inevitably destroy the morale of the best troops. Good soldiers will face any dangers and endure any hardships which promise ultimate progress, but this intermittent flinging themselves against impregnable positions breaks the stoutest hearts in the end.

There are therefore three or four considerations I wish to urge on the military situation.

1. Stalemate on the Western Front

I cannot pretend to have any military knowledge, but the little I saw and gathered in France as to the military position, coupled with such reading on the subjects as I have been able to indulge in, convinced me that any attempt to force the carefully prepared German lines in the west would end in failure and in appalling loss of life, and I then expressed this view to my colleagues. General Foch told me that there would be no more retreats on the French side, and I could well appreciate his confidence after I had driven trench behind trench from Paris all the way to the Aisne. The French generals are confident that even if the whole of the German Army now occupied in Poland were thrown on the Western Front, the French and British troops would still be able to hold their own. The same observation, of course, must apply to the German military position. We were told the other day that the Germans had, during the last few months, prepared a series of trenches of the same kind on their side right up to the Rhine. After three or four months of the most tenacious fighting, involving very heavy losses, the French have not at any point on the line gained a couple of miles. Would the throwing of an additional half-million men on this front make any real difference? To force the line you would require at least three to one; our reinforcements would not guarantee two to one, or anything approaching such a predominance. Is it not therefore better that we should recognise the impossibility of this particular task, and try and think out some way by which the distinct numerical advantage which the Allies will have attained a few months hence can be rendered effective?

2. Extension, and consequent attenuation, of enemies' front

Another consideration which ought to weigh with us is the

importance of attenuating the enemy's line by forcing him largely to extend it. The Germans now defend a front of 600 miles. No wastage in sight will so reduce their forces to such numbers as would make any part of this line untenable. . . . But if the length of the German line is doubled, even at the present rate of attrition, it might become at an early date so thin as to be easily penetrable.

3. Forcing the enemy to fight on unfavourable ground
The enemy is now fighting in country which is admirably adapted to his present intrenching tactics. He would be at a disadvantage if he were forced to fight in the open.

4. Necessity of winning a definite victory somewhere
There is another consideration which is political as well as military, but which nevertheless cannot be overlooked in an exhausting war like this, where we have to secure continuous exertion and sacrifice on the part of our people, and where we have also to think of hesitating neutrals with large armies who are still in doubt as to their action. . . . The public will soon realise that the Germans are now in effective occupation of a larger proportion of Allied territory than they were in possession of at the date of the Battle of the Aisne. This is true of Belgium, of France, and of Poland. These occupied territories contain some of the richest coalfields and industrial centres in Europe, and the most sanguinary attacks have not succeeded in moving the Germans (on an average) a single yard out of these territories. A clear definite victory which has visibly materialised in guns and prisoners captured, in unmistakable retreats of the enemy's armies, and in large sections of enemy territory occupied, will alone satisfy the public that tangible results are being achieved by the great sacrifices they are making, and decide neutrals that it is at last safe for them to throw in their lot with us.

5. An alternative suggestion
In as much as these objects cannot be accomplished by attacks on the Western Front, some alternative ought to be sought. I venture to make one or two suggestions. . . .

6. The first operation
I suggest that our new forces should be employed in an attack upon Austria, in conjunction with the Serbians, the Roumanians and the Greeks. The assistance of the two latter countries

would be assured if they knew that a great English force would be there to support them. . . .

7. *Two incidental advantages of this course*

1. Something which could be called a victory would be thus within our reach, and the public would be satisfied to support with all their resources the conduct of the War for a much longer period without grumbling or stint.

2. Italy would not only be encouraged by this formidable demonstration, she would be forced to come in in her own interest, because the operations would be conducted largely along the coast which she is looking forward to annexing to her Kingdom, as the population is predominantly Italian. . . .

8. *The second operation*

This involves an attack upon Turkey. There are four conditions which an attack on Turkey ought, in my judgment, to fulfil:

1. That it should not involve the absorption of such a large force as to weaken our offensive in the main field of operations;

2. That we should operate at a distance which would not be far from the sea, so as not to waste too many of our troops in maintaining long lines of communication and so as also to have the support of the Fleet in any eventualities;

3. That it should have the effect of forcing Turkey to fight at a long distance from her base of supplies and in country which would be disadvantageous to her;

4. That it should give us the chance of winning a dramatic victory, which would encourage our people at home, whilst it would be a corresponding discouragement to our enemies. . . .

Unless we are prepared for some project of this character I frankly despair of our achieving any success in this war. I can see nothing but an eternal stalemate on any other lines. The process of economic exhaustion alone would not bring us a triumphant peace as long as Germany is in possession of these rich allied territories. No country has ever given in under such pressure, apart from defeat in the field. Burke was always indulging in prophecies of victory as a result of France's exhaustion. The war with France went on for twenty years after he indulged in his futile predictions. Germany and Austria between them have 3,000,000 young men quite as well trained as the men of the Kitchener Armies, ready to take the place of the men now in the trenches when these fall. At that rate the process of exhaustion will take at least ten years. In soil, in minerals, in scientific equipment, Germany is a country of enormous resources. In the number of men who have a scientific training it is infinitely the richest country in the world. That must not be left out of account when we talk about the process of exhaustion. . . .

We cannot allow things to drift. We ought to look well ahead and discuss every possible project for bringing the War to a successful conclusion. Supply and ammunition difficulties, severe economic pressure, financial embarrassment, even privations and distress—nations will face them cheerfully as long as their armies in the field are in unbeaten possession of their enemies' land. But once defeat which is unmistakable comes their way, moderate economic troubles make a deep impression on their judgment. Such defeats are not to be compassed along our present lines of attack, and we ought to seek others.

If a decision were come to in favour of some such plan of campaign as I have outlined, it will take weeks to make the necessary preparations for it.

. . . It would take some time to collect the necessary intelligence as to the country, so as to decide where to land the Army and what shall be the line of attack. Transport would have to be carefully and secretly gathered. Large forces might have to be accumulated in the Mediterranean, ostensibly for Egypt. It might be desirable to send an advance force through Salonika, to assist Serbia. Military arrangements would have to be made with Roumania, Serbia, Greece and, perhaps, Italy. All this must take time. Expeditions decided upon and organised with insufficient care and preparation generally end disastrously. And as similar considerations will probably apply to any alternative campaign, I urge the importance of our taking counsel and pressing to a decision without delay.

* * *

Most of the military chiefs took the view that Germany could only be decisively defeated on the Western Front. This was the opinion of Sir Douglas Haig, who succeeded Sir John French as Commander in Chief on 15 December 1915. Haig therefore prepared to launch an offensive against the German front in 1916. The attack was delayed by the German assault on Verdun, but eventually on 1 July 1916 the British and French armies began what became known as the Battle of the Somme. The offensive continued until November 1916.

The appalling casualties and the very small advances which were made led many people to question the wisdom of such a frontal attack on the strongly defended German positions. This view was put forward by Churchill in a memorandum to the Cabinet on 1 August 1916. Haig's views are given in the extract from his Journal of 3 August 1916 and from his Despatch of 23 December 1916.

(*8c*) *From a Memorandum written for the Cabinet by Winston Churchill, 1 August 1916*
(*W. S. Churchill*—The World Crisis 1916–1918 *Part I pp 187–192, Thornton Butterworth, London, 1923*)

In personnel the results of the operation (on the Somme) have been disastrous; in terrain they have been absolutely barren. And, although our brave troops on a portion of the front, mocking their losses and ready to make every sacrifice, are at the moment elated by the small advances made and the capture of prisoners and souvenirs, the ultimate moral effect will be disappointing. From every point of view, therefore, the British offensive *per se* has been a great failure. . . .

. . . It remains to consider the effects of this tremendous and most valiant effort on the general situation in the West and other theatres. It is too early to say whether the British offensive has forced the enemy to suspend during its continuance, his costly attacks on Verdun. As soon as our offensive is definitely mastered it will be open to him either to renew them or to use his successful defence against us as a cloak or an excuse for getting out of the job. No doubt the French are pleased. Having suffered so much themselves in blood, they think it is only fair we should suffer too. Their own attack on our right was a fairly profitable operation. This is the solitary advantage in the West. Nor can it be claimed that our offensive was necessary to the Russian successes in the East. Their greatest success was gained largely by surprise before we had begun. We could have held the Germans on our front just as well by threatening an offensive as by making one. By cutting the enemy's wire, by bombardments, raiding and general activity at many unexpected points begun earlier and kept up later, we could have made it impossible for him to withdraw any appreciable force. If the French were pressed at Verdun we could have taken over more line and thus liberated reinforcements.

So long as an army possesses a strong offensive power, it rivets its adversary's attention. But when the kick is out of it, when the long-saved-up effort has been expended, the enemies' anxiety is relieved, and he recovers his freedom of movement. This is the danger into which we are now drifting.

———————

(*8d*) *From Sir Douglas Haig's Journal*
(The Private Papers of Douglas Haig *ed. R. Blake pp 157–158, Eyre and Spottiswoode, London, 1952*)

Wednesday, 3 August 1916.
. . . Note on letter received from C.I.G.S. dated 29 July.
1. 'The Powers that be' are beginning to get a little uneasy in regard to the situation.
2. Whether a loss of say 300,000 men will lead to really great results, because, if not, we ought to be content with something less than what we are now doing.
3. They are constantly enquiring why we are fighting and the French are not.
4. It is thought that the primary object—relief of pressure on Verdun—has to some extent been achieved.
I replied in AOD90 dated August 1
(a) Pressure on Verdun relieved. Not less than six enemy DIVNS. besides heavy guns have been withdrawn.
(b) Successes achieved by Russia last month would certainly have been prevented had enemy been free to transfer troops from here to the Eastern Theatre.
(c) Proof given to world that Allies are capable of making and

maintaining a vigorous offensive and of driving enemy's best troops from the strongest positions has shaken faith of Germans, of their friends, of doubting neutrals in the invincibility of Germany. Also impressed on the world, England's strength and determination, and the fighting power of the British race.

(d) We have inflicted very heavy losses on the enemy. In ONE month, 30 of his DIVNS. have beenused up, as against 35 at Verdun in 5 months. In another 6 weeks, the enemy should be hard put to it to find men.

(e) The maintenance of a steady offensive pressure will result eventually in his complete overthrow.

Principle on which we should act. MAINTAIN OUR OFFENSIVE. Our losses in July's fighting totalled about 120,000 more than they would have been had we not attacked. They cannot be regarded as sufficient to justify any anxiety as to our ability to continue the offensive. It is my intention:

(a) To maintain a steady pressure on Somme battle.

(b) To push my attack strongly whenever and wherever the state of my preparations and the general situation make success sufficiently probable to justify me in doing so, but not otherwise.

(c) To secure against counter-attack each advantage gained and prepare thoroughly for each fresh advance.

Proceeding thus, I expect to be able to maintain the offensive well into the autumn.

It would not be justifiable to calculate on the enemy's resistance being completely broken without another campaign next year.

(8e) From Sir Douglas Haig's Despatch of 23 December 1916
(Sir Douglas Haig's Despatches *ed, J. H. Boraston, pp 19–59, J. M. Dent, London, 1919*)

. . . The principle of an offensive campaign during the summer of 1916 had already been decided on by all the Allies. The various possible alternatives on the Western front had been studied and discussed by General Joffre and myself, and we were in complete agreement as to the front to be attacked by the combined French and British Armies. . . .

. . . In view of the situation in the various theatres of war, it was eventually agreed between General Joffre and myself that the combined French and British offensive should not be postponed beyond the end of June 1916.

The object of the offensive was threefold:

(i) To relieve the pressure on Verdun.

(ii) To assist our allies in other theatres of war by stopping any further transfer of German troops from the Western front.

(iii) To wear down the strength of the forces opposed to us.

The enemy's position to be attacked was of a very formidable character, situated on a high, undulating tract of ground, which rises to more than 500 feet above sea-level, and forms the watershed between the Somme on the one side and the rivers of south-western Belgium on the other. . . .

During nearly two years' preparation he (the enemy) had spared no pains to render these defences impregnable. The first and second systems each consisted of several lines of deep trenches, well provided with bomb-proof shelters and with numerous communication trenches connecting them. The front of the trenches in each system was protected by wire entanglements, many of them in two belts forty yards broad, built of iron stakes interlaced with barbed wire, often almost as thick as a man's finger.

The numerous woods and villages in and between these systems of defence had been turned into veritable fortresses. The deep cellars usually to be found in villages, and the numerous pits and quarries common to a chalk country, were used to provide cover for machine guns and trench mortars. The existing cellars were supplemented by elaborate dug-outs, sometimes in two storeys, and these were connected up by passages as much as thirty feet below the surface of the ground. The salients in the enemy's line, from which he could bring enfilade fire across his front, were made into self-contained forts, and often protected by minefields; while strong redoubts and concrete machine gun emplacements had been constructed in positions from which he could sweep his own trenches should these be taken. The ground lent itself to good artillery observation on the enemy's part, and he had skilfully arranged for cross fire by his guns.

These various systems of defence, with the fortified localities and other supporting points between them, were cunningly sited to afford each other mutual assistance and to admit of the utmost possible development of enfilade and flanking fire by machine guns and artillery. They formed, in short, not merely a series of successive lines, but one composite system of enormous depth and strength.

*   *   *

The enemy's power has not yet been broken, nor is it yet possible to form an estimate of the time the war may last before the objects for which the Allies are fighting have been attained. But the Somme battle has placed beyond doubt the ability of the Allies to gain those objects. The German Army is the mainstay of the Central Powers and a full half of that Army, despite all the advantages of the defensive, supported by the strongest fortifications, suffered defeat on the Somme this year. Neither the victors nor the vanquished will forget this; and although bad weather has given the enemy a respite, there will undoubtedly be many thousands in his ranks who will begin the campaign with little confidence in their ability to resist our assaults or to overcome our defence.

The dreadful losses suffered by the Allied armies during 1916 led to the feeling among many people that no final and complete victory could ever be achieved, and that negotiations for peace should be started. This view was most strongly expressed by Lord Lansdowne in a confidential memorandum to the Cabinet of 13 November 1916.

Lansdowne was a leading member of the Conservative Party and had strongly supported the British declaration of war in August 1914. He was Minister without Portfolio in the Coalition Government which had been formed in May 1915. The memorandum illustrates the growing feeling of frustration and hopelessness which was felt by many people at the apparently endless slaughter of the War.

After the break-up of the first Coalition in December 1916, Lansdowne ceased to be a member of the Government. He continued to hold the views expressed in this Memorandum and eventually made them public in a letter published in the *Daily Telegraph*, 29 November 1917, in which he again urged that negotiations should be started for a compromise peace with Germany.

(8f) Lord Lansdowne's Memorandum, 13 November 1916
(D. Lloyd George—War Memoirs *vol II pp 862–872, Nicholson and Watson, London, 1933–1936)*

The members of the War Committee were asked by the Prime Minister some weeks ago to express their views as to the terms upon which peace might be concluded. . . . I venture to suggest that the attention of the War Committee might with advantage be directed to a somewhat different problem, and that they should be invited to give us their opinion as to our present prospects of being able to 'dictate' the kind of terms which we should all like to impose upon our enemies if we were in a position to do so. . . .

I do not suppose for an instant that there is any weakening in the spirit of the people of this country, and I should hope, although I do not feel absolute confidence on the subject, that the same might be said of our Allies, but neither in their interests nor in ours can it be desirable that the War should be pro-

longed, unless it can be shown that we can bring it to an effectual conclusion within a resonable space of time.

What does the prolongation of the War mean?

Our own casualties already amount to over 1,100,000. We
have had 15,000 officers killed, not including those who are
missing. There is no reason to suppose that, as the force at the
front in the different theatres of war increases, the casualties
will increase at a slower rate. We are slowly but surely killing
off the best of the male population of these islands. The figures
representing the casualties of our Allies are not before me. The
total must be appalling.

. . . Generations will have to come and go before the country
recovers from the loss which it has sustained in human beings,
and from the financial ruin and the destruction of the means of
production which are taking place.

All this it is no doubt our duty to bear, but only if it can be
shown that the sacrifice will have its reward. If it is to be made
in vain, if the additional year, or two years, or three years,
finds us still unable to dictate terms, the War with its nameless
horrors will have been needlessly prolonged, and the responsibility of those who needlessly prolong such a War is not less
than that of those who needlessly provoke it.

A thorough stocktaking, first by each Ally of his own resources, present and prospective, and next by the Allies, or at
all events by the leading Allies, in confidential consultation,
seems indispensable. Not until such a stocktaking has taken
place will each Ally be able to decide which of his desiderata
are indispensable, and whether he might not be prepared to
accept less than 20s. in the £ in consideration of prompt payment. Not until it has taken place will the Allies as a body be
able to determine the broad outline of their policy or the attitude which they ought to assume towards those who talk to them
of peace.

. . . Many of us . . . must of late have asked ourselves how this
war is ever to be brought to an end. If we are told that the
deliberate conclusion of the Government is that it must be
fought until Germany has been beaten to the ground and sues
for peace on any terms which we are pleased to accord to her,
my only observation would be that we ought to know something
of the data upon which this conclusion has been reached. To

many of us it seems as if the prospect of a 'Knock-out' was, to say the least of it, remote. Our forces and those of France have shown a splendid gallantry on the Western Front, and have made substantial advances; but is it believed that these, any more than those made in 1915 with equally high hopes and accompanied by not less cruel losses, will really enable us to 'break through'? Can we afford to go on paying the same sort of price for the same sort of gains?

... I may be asked whether I have any practical suggestion to offer, and I admit the difficulty of replying. But is it not true that, unless the apprehensions which I have sketched can be shown, after such an investigation as I have suggested, to be groundless, we ought at any rate not to discourage any movement, no matter where originating, in favour of an interchange of views as to the possibility of a settlement?

... It seems to me quite inconceivable that during the winter we shall not be sounded by someone as to our readiness to discuss terms of peace or proposals for an armistice. Are we prepared with our reply? ...

9. WAR AIMS

Lloyd George's Statement of British War Aims, 5 January 1918: This speech was the fullest statement of British War aims made during the course of the War. Lloyd George had been Prime Minister since December 1916. His speech was formally approved beforehand by Asquith and Sir Edward Grey and by the Governments of the Dominions. The speech was made to a Conference of Trade Union leaders at the Caxton Hall in London, a fact which illustrates the importance which the Government attached to retaining the support of organised labour at this time. Its main purpose was to unite all classes of the community behind the Government for the final effort of the War. Lloyd George made this speech three days before President Wilson's statement of the War aims of the U.S.A.

(9a) Statement of British War Aims by Lloyd George, 5 January 1918 (D. Lloyd George—War Memoirs vol V pp 2515-2527 Nicholson and Watson, London 1933-1936)

When the Government invited organised labour in this country to assist them to maintain the might of their armies in the field, its representatives are entitled to ask that any misgivings and doubts which any of them may have about the purpose to which this precious strength is to be applied should be definitely cleared, and what is true of organised labour is equally true of all citizens in this country without regard to grade or avocation.

When men by the million are being called upon to suffer and face death and vast populations are being subjected to sufferings and privations of war on a scale unprecedented in the history of the world, they are entitled to know for what cause or causes they are making the sacrifice. It is only the clearest, greatest and justest of causes that can justify the continuance even for one day of this unspeakable agony of the nations. And we ought to be able to state clearly and definitely not only the principles for which we are fighting, but also their definite and concrete application to the war map of the world.

We have arrived at the most critical hour in this terrible conflict, and before any Government takes the fateful decision as to the conditions under which it ought either to terminate or continue the struggle, it ought to be satisfied that the conscience of the nation is behind these conditions, for nothing else can sustain the effort which is necessary to achieve a righteous end to this war. I have, therefore, during the last few days taken special pains to ascertain the view and the attitude of representative men of all sections of thought and opinion in the country. Last week I had the privilege not merely of perusing the declared war aims of the Labour Party, but also of discussing in detail with the Labour leaders the meaning and intention of that declaration. I have also had an opportunity of discussing this same momentous question with Mr Asquith and Viscount Grey. Had it not been that the Nationalist leaders are in Ireland engaged in endeavouring to solve the tangled problem of Irish self-government, I should have been happy to exchange views with them, but Mr Redmond, speaking on their behalf has, with his usual lucidity and force, in many of his speeches, made clear what his ideas are as to the object and purpose of the War. I have also had the opportunity of consulting certain representatives of the great Dominions Overseas.

I am glad to be able to say as a result of all these discussions that although the Government are alone responsible for the actual language I propose using, there is national agreement as to the character and purpose of our war aims and peace conditions, and in what I say to you today, and through you to the world, I can venture to claim that I am speaking not merely the mind of the Government but of the nation and of the Empire as a whole.

We may begin by clearing away some misunderstandings and stating what we are *not* fighting for. We are not fighting a war of aggression against the German people. Their leaders have persuaded them that they are fighting a war of self-defence against a league of evil nations bent on the destruction of Germany. That is not so. The destruction or disruption of Germany or the German people has never been a war aim with us from the first day of this war to this hour. Most reluctantly and, indeed quite unprepared for the dreadful ordeal, we were forced to join in this war in self-defence, in defence of the violated public law of Europe, and in vindication of the most solemn treaty obligations on which the public system of Europe rested, and on which Germany had ruthlessly trampled in her invasion of Belgium. We had to join in the struggle or stand aside and see Europe go under and brute force triumph over public right and international justice. It was only the realisation of that dreadful alternative that forced the British people into the War. And from that original attitude they have never swerved. They have never aimed at the break-up of the German peoples or the disintegration of their country and Empire. Germany has occupied a great position in the world. It is not our wish or intention to question or destroy that position for the future, but rather to turn her aside from the hopes and schemes of military domination and to see her devote all her strength to the great beneficent tasks of humanity. Nor are we fighting to destroy Austria-Hungary or to deprive Turkey of its capital, or of the rich and renowned lands of Asia Minor and Thrace, which are predominantly Turkish in race.

Nor did we enter this war merely to alter or destroy the Imperial constitution of Germany, much as we consider that military autocratic constitution a dangerous anachronism in the twentieth century. Our point of view is that the adoption of a really democratic constitution by Germany would be the most convincing evidence that in her the old spirit of military domination had indeed died in this war, and would make it much easier for us to conclude a broad democratic peace with her. But, after all, that is a question for the German people to decide.

* * *

The days of the Treaty of Vienna are long past. We can no longer submit the future of European civilisation to the arbitrary decisions of a few negotiators striving to secure by chicanery or persuasion the interests of this or that dynasty or nation. The settlement of the new Europe must be based on such grounds of reason and justice as will give some promise of stability. Therefore it is that we feel that government with the consent of the governed must be the basis of any territorial settlement in this war.

* * *

The first requirement, therefore, always put forward by the British Government and their Allies, has been the complete restoration, political, territorial and economic, of the independence of Belgium and such reparation as can be made for the devastation of its towns and provinces. . . .

Next comes the restoration of Serbia, Montenegro, and the occupied parts of France, Italy, and Roumania. The complete withdrawal of the alien armies and the reparation for injustice done is a fundamental condition of permanent peace.

We mean to stand by the French democracy to the death in the demand they make for a reconsideration of the great wrong of 1871, when, without any regard to the wishes of the population, two French provinces were torn from the side of France and incorporated in the German Empire. This sore has poisoned the peace of Europe for half a century. . . .

I will not attempt to deal with the question of the Russian territories now in German occupation. . . . Russia accepted war with all its horrors because, true to her traditional guardianship of the weaker communities of her race, she stepped in to protect Serbia from a plot against her independence. It is this honourable sacrifice which not merely brought Russia into the War but France as well. France, true to the conditions of her treaty with Russia, stood by her Ally in a quarrel which was not her own. Her chivalrous respect for her treaty led to the wanton invasion of Belgium; and the treaty obligations of Great Britain to that little land brought us into the War.

The present rulers of Russia are now engaged without any reference to the countries whom Russia brought into the War, in separate negotiations, with their common enemy. I am indulging in no reproaches; I am merely stating facts with a view to making it clear why Britain cannot be held accountable for decisions taken in her absence, and concerning which she has not been consulted or her aid invoked. . . . The democracy of this country means to stand to the last by the democracies of France and Italy and all our other Allies. We shall be proud to fight to the end side by side with the new democracy of Russia, so will America and so will France and Italy. But if the present rulers of Russia take action which is independent of their Allies we have no means of intervening to arrest the catastrophe which is assuredly befalling their country. Russia can only be saved by her own people.

We believe, however, that an independent Poland, comprising all those genuinely Polish elements who desire to form part of it, is an urgent necessity for the stability of Western Europe.

Similarly, though we agree with President Wilson that the

break-up of Austria-Hungary is no part of our war aims, we feel that, unless genuine self-government on true democratic principles is granted to those Austro-Hungarian nationalities who have long desired it, it is impossible to hope for the removal of those causes of unrest in that part of Europe which have so long threatened its general peace.

On the same grounds we regard as vital the satisfaction of the legitimate claims of the Italians for union with those of their own race and tongue. We also mean to press that justice be done to men of Roumanian blood and speech in their legitimate aspirations. If these conditions are fulfilled Austria-Hungary would become a Power whose strength would conduce to the permanent peace of Europe, instead of being merely an instrument for the pernicious military autocracy of Prussia that uses the resources of its allies for the furtherance of its own sinister purposes.

Outside Europe we believe that the same principles should be applied. While we do not challenge the maintenance of the Turkish Empire in the homelands of the Turkish race with its capital at Constantinople—the passage between the Mediterranean and the Black Sea being internationalised and neutralised—Arabia, Armenia, Mesopotamia, Syria and Palestine are in our judgment entitled to a recognition of their separate national conditions.

*　　*　　*

With regard to the German colonies, I have repeatedly declared that they are held at the disposal of a Conference whose decision must have primary regard to the wishes and interests of the native inhabitants of such colonies. . . . The general principle of national self-determination is therefore as applicable in their cases as in those of occupied European territories. . . .

Finally, there must be reparation for injuries done in violation of international law. The Peace Conference must not forget our seamen and the services they have rendered to, and the outrages they have suffered for, the common cause of freedom.

*　　*　　*

If, then, we are asked what we are fighting for, we reply, as we have often replied: We are fighting for a just and a lasting peace, and we believe that before permanent peace can be hoped for three conditions must be fulfilled.

First the sanctity of treaties must be re-established; secondly, a territorial settlement must be secured based on the right or self-determination or the consent of the governed; and, lastly, we must seek by the creation of some international organisation to limit the burden of armaments and diminish the probability of war.

In these conditions the British Empire would welcome peace; to secure those conditions its peoples are prepared to make even greater sacrifices than those they have yet endured.

President Wilson's Statement of War Aims 8 January 1918 (The Fourteen Points): The Fourteen Points were put forward by President Woodrow Wilson in a speech to the United States Congress on 8 January 1918. The purpose of the speech was to outline the aims for which the United States was fighting and to lay down conditions upon which peace might be made. It was on the basis of the Fourteen Points that Germany agreed to the armistice terms which were signed on 11 November 1918. The speech is also important because it contains the proposal for a 'general association of nations' which was to develop into the League of Nations.

(9b) The Fourteen Points from President Woodrow Wilson's Address to the United States Congress 8 January 1918
(A. B. Keith (ed)—Speeches and Documents on International Affairs *vol I pp 1–8, Oxford University Press, London, 1938)*

. . . It will be our wish and purpose that the processes of peace, when they are begun, shall be absolutely open, and that they shall involve and permit thenceforth no secret understandings of any kind. The day of conquest and aggrandisement is gone by; so is also the day of secret covenants entered into in the interest of particular Governments and likely at some unlooked for moment to upset the peace of the world.

It is this happy fact, now clear to the view of every public man whose thoughts do not still linger in an age that is dead and gone, which makes it possible for every nation whose purposes are consistent with justice and the peace of the world to avow now or at any other time the objects it has in view.

We entered this war because violations of right had occurred which touched us to the quick and made the life of our own people impossible unless they were corrected and the world secured once and for all against this recurrence.

What we demand in this war, therefore, is nothing peculiar to ourselves. It is that the world be made fit and safe to live in, and particularly that it be made safe for every peace-loving nation which, like our own, wishes to live its own free life, determine its own institutions, be assured of justice and fair dealing by the other peoples of the world, as against force and selfish aggression. All the peoples of the world are in effect partners in this interest, and for our own part we see very clearly that unless justice be done to others it will not be done to us.

The programme of the world's peace, therefore, is our programme, the only possible programme, as we see it, is this:

One. Open covenants of peace openly arrived at, after which there shall be no private international understandings of any kind but diplomacy shall proceed always frankly and in the public view.

Two. Absolute freedom of navigation upon the seas outside territorial waters alike in peace and in war, except as the seas may be closed in whole or in part by international action for the enforcement of international covenants.

Three. The removal, so far as possible, of all economic barriers and the establishment of an equality of trade conditions among all the nations consenting to the peace and associating themselves for its maintenance.

Four. Adequate guarantees given and taken that national armaments will be reduced to the lowest point consistent with domestic safety.

Five. A free, open-minded, and absolutely impartial adjustment of all colonial claims based upon a strict observance of the principle that in determining all such questions of sovereignty the interests of the populations concerned must have equal weight with the equitable claims of the Government whose title is to be determined.

Six. The evacuation of all Russian territory, and such a settlement of all questions affecting Russia as will secure the best and freest co-operation of the other nations of the world in obtaining for her an unhampered and unembarrassed opportunity for the independent determination of her own political development and national policy, and assure her of a sincere welcome into the society of free nations under institutions of her own choosing, and more than a welcome, assistance also of every kind that she may need and may herself desire. The treatment accorded Russia by her sister nations in the months to come will be the acid test of their goodwill, of their comprehension of her needs as distinguished from their own interests, and of their intelligent and unselfish sympathy.

Seven. Belgium, the whole world will agree, must be evacuated and restored without any attempt to limit the sovereignty which she enjoys in common with all other free nations. No other single act will serve as this will serve to restore confidence among the nations in the laws which they have themselves set and determined for the government of their relations with one another. Without this healing act the whole structure and validity of International Law is for ever impaired.

Eight. All French territory should be freed, and the invaded portions restored, and the wrong done to France by Prussia in 1871 in the matter of Alsace-Lorraine, which has unsettled the peace of the world for nearly fifty years, should be righted in order that peace may once more be made secure in the interest of all.

Nine. A readjustment of the frontiers of Italy should be effected along clearly recognisable lines of nationality.

Ten. The peoples of Austria-Hungary, whose place among the nations we wish to see safeguarded and assured, should be accorded the freest opportunity of autonomous development.

Eleven. Rumania, Serbia, and Montenegro should be evacuated, occupied territories restored, Serbia accorded free and secure access to the sea, and the relations of the several Balkan States to one another determined by friendly counsel along historically established lines of allegiance and nationality, and international guarantees of the political and economic independence and territorial integrity of the several Balkan States should be entered into.

Twelve. The Turkish portions of the present Ottoman Empire should be assured a secure sovereignty, but the other nationalities which are now under Turkish rule should be assured an undoubted security of life and an absolute unmolested opportunity of autonomous development, and the Dardanelles should be permanently opened as a free passage to the ships and commerce of all nations under international guarantees.

Thirteen. An independent Polish State should be erected which should include the territories inhabited by indisputably Polish populations, which should be assured a free and secure access to the sea, and whose political and economic independence and territorial integrity should be guaranteed by international covenant.

Fourteen. A general association of nations must be formed under specific covenants for the purpose of affording mutual guarantees of political independence and territorial integrity to great and small States alike.

In regard to these essential rectifications of wrong and assertions of right we feel ourselves to be intimate partners of all the Governments and peoples associated together against the Imperialists. We cannot be separated in interest or divided in purpose. We stand together until the end. For such arrangements and covenants we are willing to fight and to continue to fight until they are achieved, but only because we wish the right to prevail and desire a just and stable peace, such as can be secured only by removing the chief provocations to war, which this programme does remove.

We have no jealousy of German greatness and there is nothing in this programme that impairs it. We grudge her no achievement or distinction of learning or of pacific enterprise, such as have made her record very bright and very enviable. We do not wish to injure her or to block in any way her legitimate influence or power. We do not wish to fight her either with arms or with hostile arrangements of trade if she is willing to associate herself with us and the other peace-loving nations of the world in covenants of justice and law and fair-dealing. We wish her only to accept a place of equality among the peoples of the world— the new world in which we now live—instead of a place of mastery. Neither do we presume to suggest to her any alteration or modification of her institutions.

But it is necessary, we must frankly say, and necessary as a preliminary to any intelligent dealings with her on our part, that we should know whom her spokesmen speak for when they speak to us, whether for the Reichstag majority or for the military party and the man whose creed is Imperial domination.

We have spoken now surely in terms too concrete to admit of any further doubt or question. An evident principle runs through the whole programme I have outlined. It is the principle of justice to all peoples and nationalities and their right to live on equal terms of liberty and safety with one another, whether they be strong or weak.

Unless this principle be made its foundation no part of the structure of international justice can stand. The people of the United States could act upon no other principle, and to the vindication of this principle they are ready to devote their lives, their honour, and everything they possess. The moral climax of this the culminating and final war for human liberty has come, and they are ready to put their own strength, their own highest purpose, their own integrity and devotion to the test.

10. THE COVENANT OF THE LEAGUE OF NATIONS

Incorporated into each of the treaties which comprised the settlement following the First World War was the Covenant of the League of Nations. This meant that each country that signed the various treaties agreed also to the establishment of this permanent international body for the purpose of settling international disputes peaceably. Even the defeated powers, by their signatures, approved of the idea of the League, although they were not immediately permitted to join it. During the years directly following the war, there was a sincere desire on the part of all nations that mankind should never again suffer the horrors of war, and thus there was a great deal of support for the League of Nations. The only major country that did not become a member of the League of Nations was the United States. President Wilson had played a crucial part in the Peace Conference and had strongly urged the idea of an international organisation, but the United States senate refused to ratify the Treaty of Versailles and so the United States remained outside the League of Nations. The League began its work in January 1920.

THE COVENANT OF THE LEAGUE OF NATIONS

(From the Treaty of Peace between the Allied and Associated Powers and Germany 1919. H. W. V. Temperley—*The History of the Peace Conference of Paris* vol III pp. 111–123, Oxford University Press, London 1920–1924)

Part I: The Covenant of the League of Nations

The High Contracting Parties

In order to promote international co-operation and to achieve international peace and security

by the acceptance of obligations not to resort to war,

by the prescription of open, just and honourable relations between nations,

by the firm establishment of the understandings of international law as the actual rule of conduct among Governments, and

by the maintenance of justice and a scrupulous respect for all treaty obligations in the dealings of organised peoples with one another,

Agree to this Covenant of the League of Nations.

Article I

The original Members of the League of Nations shall be those of the Signatories which are named in the Annex to this Covenant and also such of those other States named in the Annex as shall accede without reservation to this Covenant. Such accession shall be effected by a declaration deposited with the Secretariat within two months of the coming into force of the Covenant. Notice thereof shall be sent to all other Members of the League.

Any fully self-governing State, Dominion or Colony not named in the Annex may become a Member of the League if its admission is agreed to by two-thirds of the Assembly, provided that it shall give effective guarantees of its sincere intention to observe its international obligations, and shall accept such regulations as may be prescribed by the League in regard to its military, naval and air forces and armaments.

Any Member of the League may, after two years' notice of its intention so to do, withdraw from the League, provided that all its international obligations and all its obligations under this Government shall have been fulfilled at the time of its withdrawal.

Article 2

The action of the League under this Covenant shall be effected through the instrumentality of an Assembly and of a Council, with a permanent Secretariat.

Article 3

The Assembly shall consist of Representatives of the Members of the League.

The Assembly shall meet at stated intervals and from time to time as occasion may require at the Seat of the League or at such other place as may be decided upon.

The Assembly may deal at its meetings with any matter within the sphere of action of the League or affecting the peace of the world.

At meetings of the Assembly each Member of the League shall have one vote, and may not have more than three Representatives.

Article 4

The Council shall consist of Representatives of the Principal

Allied and Associated Powers, together with Representatives of four other Members of the League. These four Members of the League shall be selected by the Assembly from time to time in its discretion. Until the appointment of the Representatives, the four members of the League first selected by the Assembly, Representatives of Belgium, Brazil, Spain, and Greece shall be members of the Council.

With the approval of the majority of the Assembly, the Council may name additional Members of the League whose representatives shall always be members of the Council; the Council with like approval may increase the number of members of the League to be selected by the Assembly for representation on the Council.

The Council shall meet from time to time as occasion may ·require, and at least once a year at the Seat of the League, or at such other place as may be decided upon.

The Council may deal at its meetings with any matter within the sphere of action of the League or affecting the peace of the world.

Any Member of the League not represented on the Council shall be invited to send a Representative to sit as a member at any meeting of the Council during the consideration of matters specially affecting the interests of that Member of the League.

At meetings of the Council, each Member of the League represented on the Council shall have one vote, and may have not more than one Representative.

Article 5

Except where otherwise expressly provided in this Covenant or by the terms of the present Treaty, decisions at any meeting of the Assembly or of the Council shall require the agreement of all the Members of the League represented at the meeting.

All matters of the procedure at meetings of the Assembly or of the Council, including the appointment of Committees to investigate particular matters, shall be regulated by the Assembly or by the Council and may be decided by a majority of the Members of the League represented at the meeting.

The first meeting of the Assembly and the first meeting of the Council shall be summoned by the President of the United States of America.

Article 6

The permanent Secretariat shall be established at the Seat of the League. The Secretariat shall comprise a Secretary General and such secretaries and staff as may be required.

The first Secretary General shall be the person named in the Annex; thereafter the Secretary General shall be appointed by the Council with the approval of the majority of the Assembly.

The secretaries and staff of the Secretariat shall be appointed by the Secretary General with the approval of the Council.

The Secretary General shall act in that capacity at all meetings of the Assembly and of the Council.

The expenses of the Secretariat shall be borne by the Members of the League in accordance with the apportionment of the expenses of the International Bureau of the Universal Postal Union.

Article 7

The Seat of the League is established at Geneva.

The Council may at any time decide that the Seat of the League shall be established elsewhere. All positions under or in connexion with the League, including the Secretariat, shall be open equally to men and women.

Representatives of the Members of the League and officials of the League when engaged on the business of the League shall enjoy diplomatic privileges and immunities.

The buildings and other property occupied by the League or its officials or by Representatives attending its meetings shall be inviolable.

Article 8

The Members of the League recognise that the maintenance of peace requires the reduction of national armaments to the lowest point consistent with national safety and the enforcement by common action of international obligations.

The Council, taking account of the geographical situation and circumstances of each State, shall formulate plans for such reduction for the consideration and action of the several Governments.

Such plans shall be subject to reconsideration and revision at least every ten years.

After these plans shall have been adopted by the several Governments, the limits of armaments therein fixed shall not be exceeded without the concurrence of the Council.

The Members of the League agree that the manufacture by private enterprise of munitions and implements of war is open to grave objections. The Council shall advise how the evil effects attendant upon such manufacture can be prevented, due regard being had to the necessities of those Members of the League which are not able to manufacture the munitions and implements of war necessary for their own safety.

The Members of the League undertake to interchange full and frank information as to the scale of their armaments, their military, naval and air programmes and the condition of such of their industries as are adaptable to war-like purposes.

Article 9

A permanent Commission shall be constituted to advise the Council on the execution of the provisions of Articles 1 and 8 and on military, naval and air questions generally.

Article 10

The Members of the League undertake to respect and preserve as against external aggression the territorial integrity and existing political independence of all Members of the League. In case of any such aggression or in case of any threat or danger of such aggression the Council shall advise upon the means by which this obligation shall be fulfilled.

Article 11

Any war or threat of war, whether immediately affecting any of the Members of the League or not, is hereby declared a matter of concern to the whole League, and the League shall take any action that may be deemed wise and effectual to safeguard the peace of nations. In case any such emergency should arise the Secretary General shall on the request of any Member of the League forthwith summon a meeting of the Council.

It is also declared to be the friendly right of each Member of the League to bring to the attention of the Assembly or of the Council any circumstance whatever affecting international relations which threatens to disturb international peace or good understanding between nations upon which peace depends.

Article 12

The Members of the League agree that if there should arise between them any dispute likely to lead to a rupture, they will submit the matter either to arbitration or to inquiry by the Council, and they agree in no case to resort to war until three months after the award by the arbitrators or the report by the Council.

In any case under this Article the award of the arbitrators shall be made within a reasonable time, and the report of the Council shall be made within six months after the submission of the dispute.

Article 13

The Members of the League agree that whenever any dispute shall arise between them which they recognise to be suitable for submission to arbitration and which cannot be satisfactorily settled by diplomacy, they will submit the whole subject-matter to arbitration.

Disputes as to the interpretation of a treaty, as to any question of international law, as to the existence of any fact which if established would constitute a breach of any international obligation, or as to the extent and nature of the reparation to be made for any such breach, are declared to be among those which are generally suitable for submission to arbitration.

For the consideration of any such dispute the court of arbitration to which the case is referred shall be the court agreed on by the parties to the dispute or stipulated in any convention existing between them.

The Members of the League agree that they will carry out in full good faith any award that may be rendered, and that they will not resort to war against a Member of the League which complies therewith. In the event of any failure to carry out such an award, the Council shall propose what steps should be taken to give effect thereto.

Article 14

The Council shall formulate and submit to the Members of the League for adoption plans for the establishment of a Permanent Court of International Justice. The Court shall be competent to hear and determine any dispute of an international character which the parties thereto submit to it. The Court may also give an advisory opinion upon any dispute or question referred to it by the Council or by the Assembly.

Article 15

If there should arise between Members of the League any dispute likely to lead to a rupture, which is not submitted to arbitration in accordance with Article 13, the Members of the

League agree that they will submit the matter to the Council. Any party to the dispute may effect such submission by giving notice of the existence of the dispute to the Secretary General, who will make all necessary arrangements for a full investigation and consideration thereof.

For this purpose the parties to the dispute will communicate to the Secretary General, as promptly as possible, statements of their case, with all the relevant facts and papers, and the Council may forthwith direct the publication thereof.

The Council shall endeavour to effect a settlement of the dispute, and if such efforts are successful, a statement shall be made public giving such facts and explanations regarding the dispute and the terms of settlement thereof as the Council may deem appropriate.

If the dispute is not thus settled, the Council either unanimously or by a majority vote shall make and publish a report containing a statement of the facts of the dispute and the recommendations which are deemed just and proper in regard thereto.

Any Member of the League represented on the Council may make public a statement of the facts of the dispute and of its conclusions regarding the same.

If a report by the Council is unanimously agreed to by the members thereof other than the Representatives of one or more of the parties to the dispute, the Members of the League agree that they will not go to war with any party to the dispute which complies with the recommendations of the report.

If the Council fails to reach a report which is unanimously agreed to by the members thereof, other than the Representatives of one or more of the parties to the dispute, the Members of the League reserve to themselves the right to take such action as they shall consider necessary for the maintenance of right and justice.

If the dispute between the parties is claimed by one of them, and is found by the Council, to arise out of a matter which by international law is solely within the domestic jurisdiction of that party, the Council shall so report, and shall make no recommendation as to its settlement.

The Council may in any case under this Article refer the dispute to the Assembly. The dispute shall be so referred at the request of either party to the dispute, provided that such request be made within fourteen days after the submission of the dispute to the Council.

In any case referred to the Assembly, all the provisions of this Article and of Article 12 relating to the action and powers of the Council shall apply to the action and powers of the Assembly, provided that a report made by the Assembly, if concurred in by the Representatives of those Members of the League represented on the Council and of a majority of the other Members of the League, exclusive in each case of the Representatives of the parties to the dispute, shall have the same force as a report by the Council concurred in by all the members thereof other than the Representatives of one or more of the parties to the dispute.

Article 16

Should any Member of the League resort to war in disregard of its covenants under Articles 12, 13, or 15, it shall *ipso facto* be deemed to have committed an act of war against all other Members of the League, which hereby undertake immediately to subject it to the severance of all trade or financial relations, the prohibition of all intercourse between their nationals and the nationals of the covenant-breaking State and the prevention of all financial, commercial, or personal intercourse between the nationals of the covenant-breaking State and the nationals of any other State, whether a Member of the League or not.

It shall be the duty of the Council in such case to recommend to the several Governments concerned what effective military, naval or air force the Members of the League shall severally contribute to the armed forces to be used to protect the covenants of the League.

The Members of the League agree, farther, that they will mutually support one another in the financial and economic measures which are taken under this Article, in order to minimise the loss and inconvenience resulting from the above measures, and that they will mutually support one another in resisting any special measures aimed at one of their number by the covenant-breaking State, and that they will take the necessary steps to afford passage through their territory to the forces of any of the Members of the League which are co-operating to protect the Covenants of the League.

Any Member of the League which has violated any covenant of the League may be declared to be no longer a Member of the League by a vote of the Council concurred in by the Representatives of all the other Members of the League represented thereon.

Article 17

In the event of a dispute between a Member of the League and a State which is not a Member of the League, or between States not Members of the League, the State or States not Members of the League shall be invited to accept the obligations of Membership in the League for the purposes of such dispute, upon such conditions as the Council may deem just. . . .

Article 18

Every treaty or international engagement entered into hereafter by any Member of the League shall be forthwith registered with the Secretariat and shall as soon as possible be published by it. No such treaty or international engagement shall be binding until so registered.

Article 19

The Assembly may from time to time advise the reconsideration by Members of the League of treaties which have become inapplicable and the consideration of international conditions whose continuance might endanger the peace of the world.

Article 20

The Members of the League severally agree that this Covenant is accepted as abrogating all obligations or understandings *inter se* which are inconsistent with the terms thereof, and solemnly undertake that they will not hereafter enter into any engagements inconsistent with the terms hereof. . . .

Article 21

Nothing in this Covenant shall be deemed to affect the validity of international engagements, such as treaties of arbitration or regional understandings like the Monroe Doctrine, for securing the maintenance of peace.

Article 22

To those colonies and territories which as a consequence of the late war have ceased to be under the sovereignty of the States which formerly governed them and which are inhabited by peoples not yet able to stand by themselves under the strenuous conditions of the modern world, there should be applied the principle that the well-being and development of such peoples form a sacred trust of civilisation and that securities for the performance of this trust should be embodied in this Covenant.

The best method of giving practical effect to this principle is that the tutelage of such peoples should be entrusted to advanced nations who by reason of their resources, their experience or their geographical position can best undertake this responsibility, and who are willing to accept it, and that this tutelage should be exercised by them as Mandatories on behalf of the League. . . .

In every case of mandate, the Mandatory shall render to the Council an annual report in reference to the territory committed to its charge. . . .

A permanent Commission shall be constituted to receive and examine the annual reports of the Mandatories and to advise the Council on all matters relating to the observance of the mandates.

Article 23

Subject to and in accordance with the provisions of international conventions existing or hereafter to be agreed upon, the Members of the League:

(*a*) will endeavour to secure and maintain fair and humane conditions of labour for men, women, and children, both in their own countries and in all countries to which their commercial and industrial relations extend, and for that purpose will establish and maintain the necessary international organisations.

(*b*) undertake to secure just treatment of the native inhabitants of territories under their control;

(*c*) will entrust the League with the general supervision over the execution of agreements with regard to the traffic in women and children, and the traffic in opium and other dangerous drugs;

(*d*) will entrust the League with the general supervision of the trade in arms and ammunition with the countries in which the control of this traffic is necessary in the common interest;

(*e*) will make provision to secure and maintain freedom of communications and of transit and equitable treatment for the commerce of all Members of the League. In this connexion, the special necessities of the regions devastated during the war of 1914–1918 shall be borne in mind;

(*f*) will endeavour to take steps in matters of international concern for the prevention and control of disease.

Article 24

There shall be placed under the direction of the League all international bureaux already established by general treaties if the parties to such treaties consent. All such international bureaux and all commissions for the regulation of matters of international interest hereafter constituted shall be placed under the direction of the League. . . .

Article 25

The Members of the League agree to encourage and promote the establishment and co-operation of duly authorised voluntary national Red Cross organisations having as purposes the improvement of health, the prevention of disease and the mitigation of suffering throughout the world.

Article 26

Amendments to this Covenant will take effect when ratified by the Members of the League whose representatives compose the Council and by a majority of the Members of the League whose Representatives compose the Assembly.

No such amendment shall bind any Member of the League which signifies its dissent therefrom, but in that case it shall cease to be a Member of the League.

Annex

I. Original Members of the League of Nations

U. S. of America	Cuba	Nicaragua
Belgium	Ecuador	Panama
Bolivia	France	Peru
Brazil	Greece	Poland
British Empire	Guatemala	Portugal
Canada	Haiti	Roumania
Australia	Hedjaz	Serb-Croat-Slovene State
South Africa	Honduras	Siam
New Zealand	Italy	Czecho-Slovakia
India	Japan	Uruguay
China	Liberia	

States invited to accede to the Covenant

Argentine Republic	Norway	Spain

Chili	Paraguay	Sweden
Colombia	Persia	Switzerland
Denmark	Salvador	Venezuela
Netherlands		

II. First Secretary General of the League of Nations:
The Honourable Sir James Eric Drummond, K.C.M.G., C.B.

Industrial Troubles

11. COAL INDUSTRY COMMISSION 1919

During 1919 there were continual disputes in the coal industry. The Government therefore set up a Commission to investigate the problems of the industry, with a judge, Sir John Sankey, as Chairman. The Commission, which is generally known as the Sankey Commission, was created by Act of Parliament and had power to compel the production of documents and the attendance of witnesses. It consisted of the Chairman, three miners' representatives, three coal owners, three industrialists and three economists who were acceptable to the miners. The members of the Commission failed to agree and several different reports were produced, representing the differing views. Three interim reports were produced dated 20 March 1919 and four further reports dated 20 June 1919. The extracts given below are from the reports signed by Sir John Sankey. Although seven out of the thirteen members of the Commission, including the Chairman, recommended nationalisation of the mines as the best way of dealing with the problems of the industry, the Government did not act upon their advice.

COAL INDUSTRY COMMISSION REPORT 1919

(Coal Industry Commission—Reports Cmd 359 1919)

From the Interim Report by the Honourable Mr Justice Sankey (Chairman), Mr Arthur Balfour, Sir Arthur Duckham, and Sir Thomas Royden, Bart. (20 March 1919)

I. We recommend that the Coal Mines Regulations Act 1908, commonly called the Eight Hours Act, be amended by the substitution, in the clauses limiting the hours of work underground, of the word 'seven' for the word 'eight' as and from 16 July 1919, subject to the economic position of the industry at the end of 1920, by the substitution of the word 'six' for the word 'eight' as and from 13 July 1921. Certain adjustments must be made in the hours of the classes of underground workers specifically mentioned in the Act.

II.   We recommend that as from 16 July 1919, the hours of persons employed on the surface at or about collieries shall be forty-six and a half working hours per week, exclusive of meal-times, the details to be settled locally.

III.   We recommend an increase of wages of two shillings per shift worked or per day worked in the case of the classes of colliery workers, employed in coal mines or at the pit-heads of coal mines whose wages have in the past been regulated by colliery sliding scales. In the case of workers under 16 years of age the advance is to be one shilling.

* * *

V.   The result of these Recommendations will mean:

(1) A shortening of the working day underground by one hour from 16 July 1919, and probably by a further hour from 13 July 1921.

(a) A distribution of an additional sum of £30,000,000 per annum as wages among the colliery workers.

* * *

IX.   Even upon the evidence already given, the present system of ownership and working in the coal industry stands condemned, and some other system must be substituted for it, either nationalisation or a method of unification by national purchase and/or joint control.

* * *

XV.   We are prepared however to report now that it is in the interests of the country that the colliery worker shall in the future have an effective voice in the direction of the mine. For a generation the colliery worker has been educated socially and technically. The result is a great national asset. Why not use it?

XVI.   We are further prepared to report now that the economies which should be effected by improved methods would be in the interests of the country and should result in the industry yielding even better terms for the colliery workers than those which we are at present able to recommend, and at the same time yielding a fair and just return to the capital employed.

XVII.   We think that the result of the colliery workers having an effective voice in the direction of the mine, coupled with the better terms just referred to, will enable them to reach a higher standard of living to which, in our view, they are entitled, and which many of them do not now enjoy.

*   *   *

XX.   There is one further subject which, although it forms no part of the promised Interim Report, is of so urgent a character that we feel it our duty to draw public attention to it.

XXI.   Evidence has been placed before the Commission as to the housing accommodation of the colliery workers in various districts. Although it is true that there is good housing accommodation in certain districts—and to some extent—there are houses in some districts which are a reproach to our civilisation. No judicial language is sufficiently strong or sufficiently severe to apply to their condemnation.

XXII.   It is a matter for careful consideration whether a 1d per ton should not be at once collected on coal raised and applied to improve the housing and amenities of each particular colliery district. A 1d per ton on our present output means about £1,000,000 a year.

From the Report by the Honourable Mr Justice Sankey (20 June 1919)

I.   I recommend that Parliament be invited immediately to pass legislation acquiring the Coal Royalties for the State and paying fair and just compensation to the owners.

II.   I recommend on the evidence before me that the principle of State ownership of the coal mines be accepted.

III.   I recommend that the scheme for local administration hereinafter set out, or any modification of it adopted by Parliament, be immediately set up with the aid of the Coal Controllers Department, and that Parliament be invited to pass legislation acquiring the coal mines for the State, after the scheme has been worked for three years from the date of the Report, paying fair and just compensation to the owners.

12. THE ISSUE OF PROTECTION: BALDWIN'S SPEECH AT PLYMOUTH 25 OCTOBER 1923

In this speech Stanley Baldwin, who had succeeded Bonar Law as Prime Minister in May 1923, brought the issue of Protection once more to the forefront of politics. There had been a recession in trade and the unemployment figures had been rising, but Baldwin's announcement of his belief that unemployment could only be fought by means of protective tariffs took the country and the Conservative Party by surprise. It led to an election in December 1923, which resulted in the first Labour Government coming to power.

BALDWIN'S SPEECH AT PLYMOUTH ON 25 OCTOBER 1923
(*The Times* 26 October 1923)

In connexion with the National Unionist Association Conference the Prime Minister last night addressed a large meeting in the New Palladium, Plymouth. The audience numbered nearly three thousand. Lord Mildmay of Flete was in the chair, and there were present a number of members of the Government and many other leaders of the Conservative and Unionist Party. They included Lord Selborne, Lord Peel, Lord Astor, Sir Laming Worthington-Evans, Mr Neville Chamberlain, Mr Ronald McNeill, Lord Younger of Leckie, and Mr L. S. Amery. Mr Baldwin had a great reception on reaching the platform.

The Chairman said the Prime Minister would make no fantastic promises. He would not say anything he did not mean absolutely to fulfil. (Cheers.)

Mr Baldwin said:

I thank you all for the magnificent welcome which you have given me, but I feel this evening that our first thoughts must go out to our great leader, Mr Bonar Law (Cheers), who a few years ago sacrificed his health, I might almost say his life for what he knew to be right for us and for the country. (Cheers.) I feel myself but an ineffective successor to him in experience, but I can promise you that I will do my best, and no man can do more.

*   *   *

Unemployment

... I will pass on ... to the main subject which I wish to discuss with you, the gravest subject in the country today, that of the unemployment of our people. (Cheers.) My thoughts day and night for long past have been filled with the problem, not only as Prime Minister, but as a man who for years was an employer of labour, and who has lived amongst the working people. I know what unemployment means, and no man who knows that can think of much else in these days. And almost as bad as unemployment is that apprehension of unemployment in the minds of those at work, who see the men being paid off and wonder week by week when their turn will come. It takes the spirit out of a man. No Government, no statesman, can function, can remain in power, deserves to remain in power, unless the people are convinced that everything is being done that is possible to human foresight and human wisdom.

*   *   *

But let me just say, in passing, there is one weapon, about which suggestions have been made in some quarters, which the Government is not going to use. You will no doubt have seen, as I have, suggestions for creating out of nothing artificial money to finance this, that, and the other. It is not in that way that the problem of unemployment is to be tackled. There is no truth whatever in any stories that you may hear from any quarter that any Government of which I am a member will depart from what is understood in this country to be sound financial policy. (Cheers.) It is well that this should be understood clearly at home and abroad, as great harm is being done to British credit, on which so much depends, by loose talk about inflation. (Cheers.) People are about as accurate when they talk about inflation and deflation as they are in the use of inverted commas. (Laughter.) We are not in the present circumstances, any more than we have been for many months, pursuing a policy of active deflation, and we certainly do not propose to proceed in the direction of inflation. No such project has ever been considered.

Reconstruction in Europe

I hope this will lay the ghost and now I can proceed to serious

94

business. I told you that we must consider seriously together tonight, the new facts, new since the war, an increased population in a country already industrialised to the saturation point, and secondly, we are beginning to realise now, what it was difficult to realise two years ago and what no one realised at the time of the Armistice, that it will be a long, long time before the economic reconstruction of Europe is complete. I am not going to weary you tonight with telling you what the condition of Europe means to the trade of the world and the trade of our country. You know it; but it will be years before conditions are normal, and during that time we have to find work for our people. And we have to remember this, that if, and when, such economic reconstruction is completed that Germany can pay reparations, we have to remember that whatever those reparations are, be the amount great or be it small, those reparations can only be paid by the trade balance of Germany, that is by her balance of exports.

Now, in saying this, let us not forget that Germany has lost by the Peace Treaty considerable portions of her industrial territory, which produced her raw materials, and she lost a considerable area of agricultural territory. The result is, when she begins to function economically, she will probably have to import more food and more raw materials than she did before the war, and so it follows that her exports must increase to pay for these extra imports, as well as to pay for reparations. . . . The question is, where are these exports going. . . .

The chief industrial country is ours. The country with most open market is ours, and we shall be shock-absorbers for the whole world.

. . . And I would say, in passing, that, if there were a danger— I won't say that there is a danger—but when the danger is upon us of the dumping into this country of accumulated stocks from the Ruhr to the detriment of our own manufactures, I have no doubt that Parliament, whatever party may be in power, whatever pledges may have been given, will take steps to see that no trading of the kind is allowed. (cheers).

Dealing with Mr Bonar Law's pledge given a year ago that there should be no fundamental change in the fiscal arrangements of the country, Mr Baldwin said:

That pledge binds me, and in this Parliament there will be no fundamental change. I take those words strictly: I am not a man to play with a pledge, but I cannot see myself that any slight extension or adaptation of principles hitherto sanctioned in the legislature are breaches of that pledge. But if at any time he was challenged, he was always willing to take a verdict. (Loud cheers.)

The unemployment problem was the crucial problem of our country. He regarded it as such. He could fight it. He was willing to fight it, but he could not fight it without weapons. He had come to the conclusion that if we went pottering along as we were we should have grave unemployment with us to the end of time, and he had come to the conclusion himself that the only way to fight the subject was by protecting the home market. (Prolonged cheers, and cries of 'Good old Baldwin'.) He is not a clever man. He knew nothing of political tactics, but he said this, that, having come to the conclusion himself, he felt the only honest and right thing as the Leader of a democratic party, was to tell them at the first opportunity he had what he thought, and submit it to their judgment. (Cheers.)

* * *

They were fighting something more difficult today than Germans—namely, poverty and unemployment. To fight against unemployment was vital. By its result the country would stand or fall. There could be neither peace, nor happiness, until we had got the better of unemployment. A man without employment was a man without hope or faith. Without hope or faith a man was without love—love of men, of home, and country. Love was the only power which moved the world to betterment. (Cheers.)

13. REPORT OF THE ROYAL COMMISSION ON THE COAL INDUSTRY 1925

In 1925 there was again a difficult situation in the Coal Industry. In face of European competition, British mines were running at a loss and the owners were proposing to pay lower wages and to insist on longer hours of work. This was strongly resisted by the Unions, and deadlock seemed inevitable. The Government, therefore, intervened and offered a subsidy to maintain existing wages and standard profits for a period of nine months, while a Royal Commission, under the chairmanship of Sir Herbert Samuel, investigated the problems of the industry. The Commission's terms of reference were:

'To inquire into and report upon the economic position of the Coal Industry and the conditions affecting it and to make any recommendations for the improvement thereof.'

The Samuel Commission reported on 11 March 1926. The concluding section of the Report is given here.

REPORT OF THE ROYAL COMMISSION ON
THE COAL INDUSTRY 1925

(Report of Royal Commission on the Coal Industry Cmd 2600 1925 pp 232–237)

Chapter XII: Summary of Findings and Recommendations

The coal mining industry, for more than a century the foundation of the economic strength of the country, has come upon difficult times. This change of fortune is the result of powerful economic forces. It is idle to attribute it either on the one hand to political unrest or restriction of output among the miners, or on the other hand to inefficiency in the day by day management of the mines.

At the same time we cannot agree with the view presented to us by the mine-owners that little can be done to improve the organisation of the industry, and that the only practicable course is to lengthen hours and to lower wages. In our view large changes are necessary in other directions, and large progress is possible. We agree that immediate measures are indispensable to deal with the immediate position, but the effort ought not to stop there.

The problem indeed is two-fold. It has a permanent aspect and a temporary aspect. We have proposals to make with regard to each. We will take first the permanent aspect.

The Need for Changes

The industry is marked by great diversities. Among the existing collieries many date from an earlier time, and according to modern standards are badly planned. The defects are the result partly of the age of our coalfields, partly of the private and divided ownership of the minerals, with its effects on the lay-out of the mines, partly of other causes. Very many of the collieries are on too small a scale to be good units of production. A number are defective in equipment and some in management. On the other hand there are a large number of collieries which are admirably planned, equipped and managed.

The methods of utilising coal are unscientific. Four-fifths of the coal consumed in the country is burnt in a raw state; oil and valuable by-products are wasted and the atmosphere is polluted.

Research into the methods both of winning and of using coal is inadequate.

Mining, in many places, should be intimately associated with several other industries—with gas, electricity, smokeless fuel, oil, chemical products, blast furnaces and coke ovens. A beginning has been made towards this combination, but it is no more than a beginning.

The selling organisation and the methods of transport, are too costly, and do not secure the best financial results for the collieries, and therefore for the miners employed in them.

While the relations of employers and employed are generally better than sometimes appears on the surface, the organisation of the industry on its labour side calls for many improvements.

The Proposal for Nationalisation

As a remedy for these defects the Miners' Federation propose the nationalisation of the mines. We do not recommend the adoption of this policy, for reasons which have been fully stated in this Report.

We are not satisfied that the scheme proposed to us is workable, or that it offers a clear social gain. We perceive in it grave economic dangers, and we find no advantages that cannot be obtained as readily, or more readily in other ways.

We contemplate accordingly the continuance of the industry under private enterprise, but we make a number of proposals for its reorganisation.

Recommendations on Reorganisation

1. Ownership of the Mineral.—The error which was made in times past, in allowing the ownership of the coal to fall into private hands, should be retrieved. The mineral should be acquired by the State—by purchase where it has a market value, by a declaration of State ownership in the case of unproved coal or coal at deep levels, which has now no market value. The coal of existing mines which are likely soon to cease working, and coal which is not now worked and is not likely to be developed in the future, should be excluded from the purchase. Safeguards should be adopted against excessive compensation claims. A Coal Commission should be appointed, under the authority of the Secretary for Mines, to acquire and administer the mineral property.

2. Amalgamations of existing Mines.—The amalgamation of many of the present small units of production is both desirable and practicable. This may often be effected from within, but in many cases it will only take place if outside assistance is given. Any general measure of compulsory amalgamation, on arbitrary lines, would be mischievous; the action to be taken should be elastic and should enable each case to be treated individually. The State as mineral owner will be able to promote desirable amalgamations when granting new leases or renewing old ones. Legislation should provide for a compulsory transfer of interests under existing leases where desirable amalgamations are prevented by the dissent of some of the parties or their reasonable claims. Existing leases would not otherwise be affected.

3. Combination of Industries.—A closer connection of mining with the allied industries should be promoted. Highly technical questions are involved, affecting a number of industries, and not electricity alone. The development of electrical supply under the new proposals of the Government should be closely co-ordinated with the generation of electricity at the mines. The heat, power

and light requirements of the country should be under the constant and comprehensive survey of a body formed for the purpose. We propose for consideration the establishment of a National Fuel and Power Committee, with advisory powers, composed of representatives nominated by the Government from among the official and other bodies concerned.

4. Research.—The existing provision for research should be largely extended by the industry with the support of the State. It is urgently necessary that new methods for winning and utilising coal should be sought for, and should be found, if the prosperity of the industry is to be restored and a proper standard of wages and working conditions assured to the workers. If processes of low temperature carbonisation were perfected, great national advantages would ensue, particularly through the production of a smokeless fuel for domestic and industrial use, and the provision of large supplies of mineral oil from the country's own resources. The State should give financial support to the further experiments, on a commercial scale, which are necessary.

5. Distribution.—The industry as a whole has so far failed to realise the benefits to be obtained by a readiness to co-operate. Large financial advantages might be gained by the formation, in particular, of co-operative selling agencies. They are specially needed in the export trade.

The Government should consider the establishment of an official system for the sampling and analysis of coal, with a view to encouraging selling on specification and guarantee, in both the home and the foreign markets.

Local authorities should be empowered to engage in the retail sale of coal.

We propose measures to secure the adoption of larger mineral wagons on the railways, and a greater concentration of ownership of wagons. A Standing Joint Committee of the Ministry of Transport and the Mines Department should be formed to promote these measures.

6. Labour.—The relations between employers and employed are of fundamental importance, and here also we are convinced that a number of changes are necessary.

(1) The principle on which the recent wage-agreements have been based is in our opinion sound, but amendments are needed

in the method of ascertaining the proceeds of the industry for the fixing of wages. A large proportion of the coal is sold by the mines to associated industries, and the most important of these amendments relates to the prices at which these transfers are made.

(2) The standard length of the working day, which is now on the average 7½ hours underground, should remain unaltered. The optional redistribution of hours within the present weekly total, over a week of five days instead of six, should be considered. The multiple shift system should be extended.

(3) Joint pit committees should be established generally.

(4) The methods of payment of men not employed at the face should be revised where possible so as to give them a direct interest in output.

(5) The introduction of a family allowance system either nationally or by districts is desirable. Pooling schemes should be adopted to prevent married men with families being prejudiced in obtaining employment.

(6) Profit-sharing schemes, providing for the distribution to the workmen of shares in the undertakings, should be generally adopted in the industry, and should be made obligatory by statute.

(7) For all new collieries, a proper provision of houses for the workers should be a condition of the lease.

(8) The general establishment of pit-head baths is necessary. This should be undertaken by the existing Miners' Welfare Fund, which should be increased by a substantial contribution from royalties.

(9) When prosperity returns to the industry we consider that annual holidays with pay should be established.

The Immediate Problem

To bring any of these measures of reorganisation into effect must need a period of months; to bring all of them into full operation must need years. The Miners' Federation fully recognise that, even if nationalisation were to be accepted, much time must elapse before the great changes it involves could be put into force and the effects be seen. Meantime the hard economic conditions of the moment remain to be faced.

The dominant fact is that, in the last quarter of 1925, if the subsidy be excluded, 73 per cent of the coal was produced at a loss.

We express no opinion whether the grant of a subsidy last July was unavoidable or not, but we think its continuance indefensible. The subsidy should stop at the end of its authorised term, and should never be repeated.

We cannot approve the proposal of the Mining Association, that the gap between costs and proceeds should be bridged by an increase of an hour in the working day, reductions in the miners' wages, some economies in other costs, and a large diminution in railway rates to be effected by lowering the wages of railwaymen. In any case these proposals go beyond the need, for we do not concur in the low estimate of future coal prices on which they are based.

While the mine-owners presented a plan which is unacceptable, the Miners' Federation abstained from making any suggestion as to the means for meeting the immediate situation. The duty therefore devolves upon the Commission to formulate its own proposals.

If the present hours are to be retained, we think a revision of the 'minimum percentage addition to standard rates of wages,' fixed in 1924 at a time of temporary prosperity, is indispensable. A disaster is impending over the industry, and the immediate reduction of working costs that can be effected in this way, and in this way alone, is essential to save it. The minimum percentage is not a 'minimum wage' in the usual sense of that term. The wages of the lowest paid men will be safeguarded by the continuance of the system of subsistence allowances. The reductions that we contemplate will still leave the mine-owners without adequate profits in any of the wage-agreement districts, and without any profits in most districts. If trade improves and prices rise, a profit will be earned. If prices do not rise, an adequate profit must be sought in the improved methods which should in any case be adopted.

Should the miners freely prefer some extension of hours with a less reduction of wages, Parliament would no doubt be prepared to authorise it. We trust, however, that this will not occur.

We consider that it is essential that there should be, as there always has been hitherto, considerable variation in the rates of wages in the several districts. But we are strongly of opinion that national wage agreements should continue. Such agreements are entered into in all the other British industries of importance.

We recommend that the representatives of the employers and employed should meet together, first nationally and then in the districts, in order to arrive at a settlement by the procedure that we have previously suggested.

By a revision of the minimum percentage coal mining would be saved from an immediate collapse, but it seems inevitable that a number of collieries would still have to be closed. This may give rise to the necessity for a transfer of labour on a considerable scale. We recommend that the Government should be prepared in advance with such plans to assist it as are practicable, and should provide funds for the purpose.

Conclusion

In the summer of last year the nation was oppressed by a grave anxiety. Having emerged from the mental stress and the economic strain of an unprecedented war, aware of the imperative need of recuperating its strength, it found itself faced by the possibility of an industrial conflict, or a series of conflicts, on a scale equally unprecedented, perhaps, in extent and in duration. And the issues that were at stake were wider even than the limits of the nation; for the stability and the prosperity of Great Britain have a profound influence both upon the opinion and upon the interests of Europe, and of the world at large. If there were here a period of confusion and conflict, of instability and retrogression, the effects would be felt in a widening circle everywhere else.

This Commission was appointed to investigate the causes of the trouble and to endeavour to suggest a remedy. We have discharged our onerous duty to the best of our ability. There is no part of this wide field which we have not sought to examine. We have suggested a series of definite constructive proposals.

The way to prosperity for the mining industry lies along three chief lines of advance: through greater application of science to the winning and using of coal, through larger units for production and distribution, through fuller partnership between employers and employed. In all three respects progress must come mainly from within the industry. The State can help materially—by substantial payments in aid of research; by removing obstacles to amalgamation under existing leases; as owner of the minerals by determining the conditions of new leases; by legislation for the establishment of pit committees and of profit-sharing, and in other ways.

The future depends primarily upon the leadership, and the general level of opinion, among the mine-owners and the miners of Great Britain. In laying down our charge, we would express our own firm conviction, that if the present difficulties be wisely handled, if the grievances of the one side and of the other be remedied, and a better spirit prevail in consequence between them, the mining industry, with the aid of science, will certainly recover, and even surpass, its former prosperity. It will again become a source of great economic strength to the nation.

All which we humbly submit for Your Majesty's gracious consideration.

HERBERT SAMUEL (*Chairman*)   C. S. HURST (*Secretary*)

H. A. LAWRENCE   F. C. STARLING

W. H. BEVERIDGE   (*Assistant Secretary*)

KENNETH LEE   *6 March 1926*

14. THE T.U.C. MEMORANDUM ON THE GENERAL STRIKE 1 MAY 1926

The Government agreed to implement the proposals of the Samuel Commission Report, provided that both the mine-owners and the miners would agree to accept these proposals. The Government subsidy to the coal industry was to end on 30 April. Despite long negotiations no agreement was reached. The mine-owners insisted that there must be a reduction in wages and an extension of the working day; the miners' attitude was summed up in the phrase of A. J. Cook, the Secretary of the Miners' Federation: 'Not a penny off the pay, not a minute on the day.' The miners were supported by the Trades Union Congress. On Saturday, 1 May, the Trade Unions agreed on 'co-ordinated action', and that this action should begin at midnight on Monday, 3 May. The following memorandum, which had been drawn up by Ernest Bevin and Arthur Purcell, was then issued to the unions.

THE T.U.C. MEMORANDUM ON THE GENERAL STRIKE 1 MAY 1926

(W. Milne-Bailey (ed)—*Trade Union Documents* pp 342–344 Bell, London 1929)

The Trades Union Congress General Council and the Miners' Federation of Great Britain, having been unable to obtain a satisfactory settlement of the matters in dispute in the coal mining industry, and the Government and the mine-owners having forced a lock-out, the General Council, in view of the need for co-ordinated action on the part of the affiliated Unions, in defence of the policy laid down by the General Council of the Trades Union Congress, directs as follows:

1. Trades and Undertakings to Cease Work.

Except as hereinafter provided, the following trades and undertakings shall cease work as and when required by the General Council:

Transport, including all affiliated Unions connected with transport, i.e. railways, sea transport, docks, wharves, harbours, canals, road transport, railway repair shops; and contractors for railways and all Unions connected with the maintenance of, or equipment, manufacturing, repairs and groundsmen employed in connection with air transport.

Printing Trades including the Press.

Productive Industries, Iron and Steel, Metal, and Heavy Chemical Group, including all metal workers and other workers who are engaged or may be engaged in installing alternative plant to take the place of coal.

Building Trade—all workers engaged on building, except such as are employed definitely on housing and hospital work, together with all workers engaged in the supply of equipment to the Building Industry shall cease work.

Electricity and Gas—The General Council recommend that the Trade Unions connected with the supply of electricity and gas shall co-operate with the object of ceasing to supply power. The Council request that the Executives of the Trades Unions concerned shall meet at once with a view to formulating common policy.

Sanitary Services.—The General Council direct that sanitary services be continued.

Health and Food Services.—The General Council recommend that there should be no interference in regard to these, and that the Trade Unions concerned should do everything in their power to organise the distribution of milk and food to the whole of the population.

With regard to hospitals, clinics, convalescent homes, sanatoria, infant welfare centres, maternity homes, nursing homes, schools, the General Council direct that affiliated Unions take every opportunity to ensure that food, milk, medical and surgical supplies shall be efficiently provided.

2. Trade Union Discipline.—(a) The General Council direct that, in the event of Trade Unionists being called upon to cease work, the Trade Unions concerned shall take steps to keep a daily register to account for every one of their members. It should be made known that any workers called upon to cease work should not leave their own district, and by following another occupation, or the same occupation in another district, blackleg their fellow workers. (b) The General Council recommend that the actual calling out of the workers should be left to the Unions, and instructions should only be issued by the ac-

credited representatives of the Unions participating in the dispute.

3. Trades Councils.—The work of the Trades Councils, in conjunction with the local officers of the Trade Unions actually participating in the dispute, shall be to assist in carrying out the foregoing provisions, and they shall be charged with the responsibility of organising the Trade Unionists in dispute in the most effective manner for the preservation of peace and order.

4. Incitement to Disorder and Spies.—A strong warning must be issued to all localities that any person found inciting the workers to attack property or inciting the workers to riot must be dealt with immediately. It should be pointed out that the opponents will in all probability employ persons to act as spies and others to use violent language in order to incite the workers to disorder.

5. Trade Union Agreements.—The General Council further direct that the Executives of the Unions concerned shall definitely declare that in the event of any action being taken and Trade Union agreements being placed in jeopardy, it be definitely agreed that there will be no general resumption of work until those agreements are fully recognised.

6. Procedure.—(a) These proposals shall be immediately considered by the Executives of the Trade Unions concerned in the stoppage, who will at once report as to whether they will place their powers in the hands of the General Council and carry out the instructions which the General Council may issue from time to time concerning the necessary action and conduct of the dispute.

(b) And, further, that the Executives of all other affiliated Unions are asked to report at once as to whether they will place their powers in the hands of the General Council and carry out the instructions of the General Council from time to time, both regarding the conduct of the dispute and financial assistance.

Signed   A. PUGH, *Chairman*
      WALTER M. CITRINE,
          Acting Secretary

15. DIFFERING VIEWS ON
THE GENERAL STRIKE

The General Strike lasted from 3 May to 12 May 1926. During this period newspapers, if able to publish at all, could only produce very small, emergency editions. The Government published the *British Gazette*, edited by Winston Churchill, as the official Government newspaper, and in reply, the *British Worker* was published by the General Council of the Trades Union Congress. The following extracts give an indication of some of the views expressed by the newspapers during the Strike.

(*15a*) Daily Herald *4 May 1926*

The miners are locked out to enforce reductions of wages and an increase in hours. The Government stands behind the mine-owners. It has rebuffed the Trade Union Movement's every effort to pave the way to an honourable peace.

The renewed conversations begun on Saturday were ended abruptly in the early hours of yesterday morning, with an ultimatum from the Cabinet. Despite this, the whole Labour Movement, including the miners' leaders, continued its efforts yesterday.

But unless a last minute change of front by the Government takes place during the night the country will today be forced, owing to the action of the Government, into an industrial struggle bigger than this country has yet seen.

In the Commons Mr Baldwin showed no sign of any receding from his attitude that negotiations could not be entered into if the General Strike order stood and unless reductions were accepted before negotiations opened.

In reply Mr J. H. Thomas declared that the responsibility for the deadlock lay with the Government and the owners, and that the Labour Movement was bound in honour to support the miners in the attacks on their standard of life.

Both from the debate in the Commons yesterday, and from the long and patient efforts of the Trade Union Movement, the central fact stands out that the blame for the crisis rests on the Government and the mine-owners.

* * *

108

The General Council of the Trades Union Congress last night issued the following message:

The Trade Unions are fighting in defence of the mine-workers. The responsibility for the national crisis lies with the Government.

With the people the trade unions have no quarrel. On the contrary, the unions are fighting to maintain the standard of life of the great mass of the people.

The trade unions have not entered upon this struggle without counting the cost. They are assured that the trade unionists of the country, realising the justice of the cause they are called upon to support, will stand loyally by their elected leaders until the victory and an honourable peace has been won.

The need now is for loyalty, steadfastness and unity.

The General Council of the Trade Union Congress appeals to the workers to follow the instructions that have been issued by their union leaders.

Let none be disturbed by rumours or be driven by panic to betray the cause.

Violence and disorder must be everywhere avoided no matter what the incitement.

Stand firm and we shall win.

(*15b*) The Times *6 May 1926*

A general strike having been proclaimed, and being to some extent in force, the nation are called upon to support the constitutional Government which they themselves placed in power by huge majorities. The duty to obey the call is manifest, and there is already evidence that they will perform it with alacrity and with resolve. They will not patiently suffer any self-constituted authority, however well organised, to supersede Parliament and to override the will of the people. . . . No Government worthy of the name can give it the slightest countenance, or dream of abdicating into other hands duties and responsibilities entrusted to them—and to them only—by the Constitution and by the people. The people would have no pardon for such a breach of trust. . . .

They have followed with hearty sympathy and with warm admiration the unflagging efforts of their Government to bring about a peaceful settlement of the controversy and to avert the ruin of a general strike. The nation has shown its confidence in trade unionism and its approbation of trade unionism when trade unionism has been conducted upon reasonable principles and upon constitutional lines. . . . But goodwill and sympathy cannot blind its judgment to the fact that a general strike inflicts a grievous injury upon the community as a whole. They are committing a high offence and a dangerous offence against the nation and neither sympathy nor goodwill will prevent the nation from reprobating this misdeed as it deserves.

(*15c*) *The* British Gazette *6 May 1926*
(*The official Government newspaper published by His Majesty's Stationery Office*)

The General Strike is in operation, expressing in no uncertain terms a direct challenge to ordered government. It would be futile to attempt to minimise the seriousness of such a challenge, constituting as it does an effort to force upon some 42,000,000 British citizens the will of less than 4,000,000 others engaged in the vital services of the country.

The strike is intended as a direct hold-up of the nation to ransom. It is for the nation to stand firm in its determination not to flinch. 'This moment,' as the Prime Minister pointed out in the House of Commons, 'has been chosen to challenge the existing Constitution of the country and to substitute the reign of force for that which now exists. . . . I do not believe there has been anything like a thorough-going consultation with the rank and file before this despotic power was put into the hands of a small executive in London. . . . I do not think all the leaders who assented to order a general strike fully realised that they were threatening the basis of ordered government and coming nearer to proclaiming civil war than we have been for centuries past.'

(*15d*) *The* British Worker *7 May 1926*
(*The Official Strike News Bulletin published by the The General Council of the Trades Union Congress*)

The General Council does not challenge the Constitution. It is not seeking to substitute unconstitutional government. Nor is it desirous of undermining our Parliamentary institutions. The sole aim of the Council is to secure for the miners a decent standard of life. The Council is engaged in an Industrial Dispute. There is no Constitutional crisis. . . .

It is . . . fantastic for the Prime Minister to pretend that the Trade Unions are engaged in an attack upon the Constitution of the Country. Every instruction issued by the General Council is evidence of their determination to maintain the struggle strictly on the basis of an industrial dispute. They have ordered every member taking part to be exemplary in his conduct and not to give any cause for police interference. The General Council struggled hard for peace. They are anxious that an honourable peace shall be secured as soon as possible. They are not attacking the Constitution. They are not fighting the community. They are defending the mine workers against the mine-owners.

16. THE END OF THE GENERAL STRIKE: THE SAMUEL MEMORANDUM 10 MAY 1926

This Memorandum was drawn up by Sir Herbert Samuel in consultation with the Trade Union leaders. Its aim was to break the deadlock between the Trade Unions and the Government and to get negotiations started once more. The Memorandum was accepted by the Trades Union Congress as a basis for reopening negotiations and calling off the General Strike. The miners, however, refused to accept it. On 12 May the General Council of the T.U.C. ended the General Strike unconditionally. The miners continued the strike throughout the summer but were finally compelled to return to work and to accept longer hours and lower wages.

THE SAMUEL MEMORANDUM 10 MAY 1926

(W. Milne-Bailey (ed)—*Trade Union Documents* pp 348–350
Bell, London 1929)

1. The negotiations upon the condition of the coal industry should be resumed, the subsidy being renewed for such reasonable period as may be required for that purpose.

2. Any negotiations are unlikely to be successful unless they provide for means of settling disputes in the industry other than conferences between the mine-owners and the miners alone. A National Wages Board should, therefore, be established, which would include representatives of those two parties, with a neutral element and an independent chairman. The proposals in this direction tentatively made in the report of the Royal Commission should be pressed, and the powers of the proposed board enlarged.

3. The parties to the Board should be entitled to raise before it any points they consider relevant to the issue under discussion, and the Board should be required to take such points into consideration.

4. There should be no revision of the previous wage rates, unless there are sufficient assurances that the measures of reorganisation proposed by the Committee will be effectively adopted. A Committee should be established as proposed by the Prime Minister, on which representatives of the men should be included, whose duty it should be to co-operate with the Govern-

ment in the preparation of the legislative and administrative measures that are required. The same Committee or alternatively, the National Wages Board, should assure itself that the necessary steps, so far as they relate to matters within the industry, are not being neglected or unduly postponed.

5. After these points have been agreed and the Mine National Wages Board has considered every practicable means of meeting such immediate financial difficulties as exist, it may, if that course is found to be absolutely necessary, proceed to the preparation of a wage agreement.

6. Any such agreement should

(i) If practicable be on simpler lines than those hitherto followed.

(ii) Not adversely affect in any way the wages of the lowest paid men.

(iii) Fix reasonable figures below which the wage of no class of labour, for a normal customary week's work, should be reduced in any circumstances.

(iv) In the event of any new adjustments being made, should provide for the revision of such adjustments by the Wages Board from time to time if the facts warrant that course.

7. Measures should be adopted to prevent the recruitment of new workers, over the age of 18 years, into the industry if unemployed miners are available.

8. Workers who are displaced as a consequence of closing of uneconomic collieries should be provided for by

(a) The transfer of such men as may be mobile, with the Government assistance that may be required, as recommended in the Report of the Royal Commission.

(b) The maintenance, for such period as may be fixed, of those who cannot be so transferred, and for whom alternative employment cannot be found; this maintenance to comprise an addition to the existing rate of unemployment pay under the Unemployment Insurance Act, of such amount as may be agreed. A contribution should be made by the Treasury to cover the additional sums so disbursed.

(c) The rapid construction of new houses to accommodate transferred workers. The Trades Union Congress will facilitate this by consultation and co-operation with all those who are concerned.

17. TRADE DISPUTES
AND TRADE UNION ACT 1927

The Cabinet had decided during the General Strike that the law concerning strikes should be changed. Debate on the subject occupied most of May 1927. In spite of very strong opposition from the Labour Party and from the Trade Union movement, the Bill was passed and became law in July 1927. The Act declared illegal any general or sympathetic strike, though the clause was never invoked. It also had the effect of reducing very considerably the Labour Party's income by stipulating that members of unions who wished to pay the political levy had to 'contract in' instead of, as previously, being required to 'contract out' of such payments. The Act continued to be very unpopular with the Labour Party and the Trade Unions and it prolonged and strengthened the bitterness caused by the General Strike. It was repealed by the Labour Government in 1946.

TRADE DISPUTES AND TRADE UNION ACT 1927

(Public General Acts 17–18 Geo 5 c 22)

An Act to declare and amend the law relating to trade disputes and trade unions, to regulate the position of civil servants and persons employed by public authorities in respect of membership of trade unions and similar organisations, to extend section five of the Conspiracy, and Protection of Property Act, 1875, and for other purposes connected with the purposes aforesaid.

(29 July 1927)

Be it enacted . . . as follows:

1. (1) It is hereby declared—

    (a) that any strike is illegal if it—

        (i) has any object other than or in addition to the furtherance of a trade dispute within the trade or industry in which the strikers are engaged; and

        (ii) is a strike designed or calculated to coerce the Government either directly or by inflicting hardship upon the community; and

    (b) that any lock-out is illegal if it—

        (i) has any object other than or in addition to the furtherance of a trade dispute within the trade or industry in which the employers locking-out are engaged; and

(ii) is a lock-out designed or calculated to coerce the Government either directly or by inflicting hardship upon the community:

and it is further declared that it is illegal to commence, or continue, or to apply any sums in furtherance or support of, any such illegal strike or lock-out.

For the purposes of the foregoing provisions—

(a) a trade dispute shall not be deemed to be within a trade or industry unless it is a dispute between employers and workmen or between workmen and workmen, in that trade or industry which is connected with the employment or non-employment or the terms of employment, or with the conditions of labour, of persons in that trade or industry; and

(b) without prejudice to the generality of the expression 'trade or industry' workmen shall be deemed to be within the same trade or industry if their wages or conditions of employment are determined in accordance with the conclusions of the same joint industrial council, conciliation board or other similar body, or in accordance with agreements made with the same employer or group of employers.

(2) If any person declares, instigates, incites others to take part in or otherwise acts in furtherance of a strike or lock-out, declared by this Act to be illegal, he shall be liable on summary conviction to a fine not exceeding ten pounds or to imprisonment for a term not exceeding three months, or on conviction on indictment to imprisonment for a term not exceeding two years.

Provided that no person shall be deemed to have committed an offence under this section or at common law by reason only of his having ceased work or refused to continue to work or to accept employment.

2. (1) No person refusing to take part or to continue to take part in any strike or lock-out which is by this Act declared to be illegal, shall be, by reason of such refusal or by reason of any action taken by him under this section, subject to expulsion from any trade union or society, or to any fine or penalty, or to deprivation of any right or benefit to which he or his legal personal representatives would otherwise be entitled, or liable

to be placed in any respect either directly or indirectly under any disability or at any disadvantage as compared with other members of the union or society, anything to the contrary in the rules of a trade union or society notwithstanding.

(2) No provisions of the Trade Union Acts 1871 to 1917, limiting the proceedings which may be entertained by any court, and nothing in the rules of a trade union or society requiring the settlement of disputes in any manner shall apply to any proceeding for enforcing any right or exemption secured by this section, and in any such proceeding the court may, in lieu of ordering a person who has been expelled from membership of a trade union or society to be restored to membership, order that he be paid out of the funds of the trade union or society such sum by way of compensation or damages as the court thinks just.

(3) As respects any strike or lock-out before the passing of this Act but since the first day of May, nineteen hundred and twenty-six, which, according to the law as declared by this Act, was illegal, this section shall have effect as if it had been in operation when the strike or lock-out took place.

3.   (1) It is hereby declared that it is unlawful for one or more persons . . . to attend at or near a house or place where a person resides or works or carries on business or happens to be, for the purpose of obtaining or communicating information or of persuading or inducing any person to work or to abstain from working, if they so attend in such numbers or otherwise in such manner as to be calculated to intimidate any person in that house or place, or to obstruct the approach thereto or the egress therefrom, or to lead to a breach of the peace; . . .

(2) In this section the expression 'to intimidate' means to cause in the mind of a person a reasonable apprehension of injury to him or to any member of his family or to any of his dependants or of violence or damage to any person or property, and the expression 'injury' includes injury to a person in respect of his business, occupation, employment or other source of income, and includes any actionable wrong.

*   *   *

4.   (1) It shall not be lawful to require any members of a trade union to make any contribution to the political fund of a trade

union unless he has at some time after the commencement of this Act, and before he is first after the thirty-first day of December, nineteen hundred and twenty-seven, required to make such a contribution delivered at the head office or some branch office of the trade union, notice in writing . . . of his willingness to contribute to that fund and has not withdrawn the notice in manner hereinafter provided; and every member of a trade union who has not delivered such a notice as aforesaid, or who, having delivered such a notice, has withdrawn it in manner hereinafter provided, shall be deemed for the purposes of the Trade Union Act 1913, to be a member who is exempt from the obligation to contribute to the political fund of the union . . .

(2) All contributions to the political fund of a trade union from members of the trade union who are liable to contribute to that fund shall be levied and made separately from any contributions to the other funds of the trade union . . .

5. (1) Amongst the regulations as to the conditions of service in His Majesty's civil establishments there shall be included regulations prohibiting established civil servants from being members, delegates or representatives of any organisation of which the primary object is to influence or affect the remuneration and conditions of employment of its members, unless the organisation is an organisation of which the membership is confined to persons employed by or under the Crown and is an organisation which complies with such provisions as may be contained in the regulations for securing, that it is in all respects independent of, and not affiliated to, any such organisation as aforesaid the membership of which is not confined to persons employed by or under the Crown or any federation comprising such organisations, that its objects do not include political objects, and that it is not associated directly or indirectly with any political party or organisation . . .

18. REPORT OF THE ROYAL COMMISSION ON UNEMPLOYMENT INSURANCE 1931–1932

One of the most difficult problems which faced British governments in the years between the wars was the problem of unemployment. The Labour Government of 1929 to 1931 was confronted with rapidly rising unemployment. In July 1930 there were some 2 million unemployed in Great Britain, and by December 1930 the number had risen to 2½ million. The provision for Unemployment Insurance benefits threatened to break down because of the vast numbers of unemployed people making demands upon it. In an effort to remedy this situation the Government appointed a Royal Commission in December 1930 under the Chairmanship of Mr Justice Holman Gregory 'To enquire into the provisions and working of the Unemployment Insurance Scheme and to make recommendations.' The Commission produced two reports, the first in June 1931 and the second in November 1932. The following extracts are taken from the First Report.

ROYAL COMMISSION ON UNEMPLOYMENT INSURANCE

(*First Report* June 1931 Cmd 3872 *Second Report* November 1932 Cmd 4185)

* * *

12. The average percentage of the insured population recorded as unemployed at the end of each month since December 1920 when the Unemployment Insurance Scheme was extended to its present limits, is 12.2; representing nearly one and a half million persons. . . .

* * *

18. The causes of the depression in the industries of exceptional unemployment are easy to understand. These industries fall into three broad classes which, to some extent, overlap. There is first, the class of industry which is still suffering from a war-time expansion in excess of normal peace-time requirements. . . . In this class fall iron and steel, shipbuilding and certain branches of engineering, and to some extent, coalmining. There is second, the class of industry that before the war was dependent to a great extent on exports, and that has suffered since the war a loss

of part of its overseas markets, coupled in some cases with an invasion by imports of its home market. This is the largest class, overlapping the previous class, and accounting most obviously for the exceptional unemployment in the textile and coal-mining industries. There is a third, a class of industries, which has been expanding rather than contracting and enjoying in some cases a high degree of prosperity in which, in the words of the Ministry of Labour's Memorandum of Evidence, 'the extent of recorded unemployment is almost as much a matter of internal organisation as of external pressure of bad trade. . . .' To this class belong building and public works contracting, in which a large expenditure of public money has stimulated employment without preventing unemployment; docks; and the expanding service of road transport.

* * *

20. It is clear . . . that the most serious element in the situation is the average level of unemployment of 12.2 per cent. This represents a persistent and obdurate problem, and, in our view it would be unwise to treat this experience of the last ten years as transitory or to assume that it over-values the risk that has to be provided for in the next few years. Moreover, for the purpose of immediate measures, it must be noted that the percentage of unemployment today is, in fact, far higher than 12.2 per cent; since December 1930 it has been 20 per cent or over. This excess over average is due to . . . the world wide depression of the last eighteen months. The indications are that unemployment will not fall appreciably in the next few months below the present level. What is necessary now is to adjust the finances of the Fund to present circumstances, and for the purposes of this Report we do not feel justified in anticipating an average Live Register (of unemployed persons) of less than 2,500,000.

* * *

65. Under present conditions the income and expenditure of the Unemployment Fund balance when 900,000 persons are qualified for Insurance benefit. The decrease in contribution income is about £350,000 per annum for each 100,000 persons added to the Live Register while the increase in benefit paid is about

£4,500,000. Assuming that the average Live Register is 2,500,000 the annual income of the Fund by contributions in respect of employed persons is as follows:

From employers	£15,650,000
From employed persons	13,650,000
From the Exchequer	14,850,000
Other receipts	400,000
	£44,550,000

66. The corresponding payments for Insurance benefit are estimated to amount to:

To the claimant	£61,250,000
Additional payment for dependents	13,250,000
Cost of administration	5,000,000
Interest on debt	4,500,000
	£84,000,000

67. . . . . At this rate of unemployment, the beneficiaries are drawing out of the Unemployment Fund more than two and a half times the amount paid in contributions by employers and workers. . . .

*   *   *

129. The following is a summary of the measures which we recommend to deal with the present situation pending our final Report.

I. THE UNEMPLOYMENT INSURANCE SCHEME

In order that the income and expenditure of the Unemployment Fund may be brought more closely to balancing point with a Live Register of 2,500,000 we recommend:

(1) A limit upon the period for which benefit may be paid of 26 weeks within the period of 12 months following the date of application.

(2) An increase in the weekly rates of contributions so that, in the case of the adult man, each of the three parties (the

worker, the employer and the Exchequer) pays 9d, with appropriate increases in the rates of contribution for other classes.

(3) An amendment of the weekly rates of unemployment benefit in accordance with the following scale:

Ordinary Rates of Benefit

Age	Males	Females
Over 21	15/–	13/–
18–21	12/–	10/–
17–18	7/–	6/–
16–17	5/–	5/–

Dependents Benefit

Rate of additional benefit for an adult dependent, 8/– per week.
Rate of additional benefit for a dependent child, 2/– per week.

19. THE UNEMPLOYMENT INSURANCE ACT 1934

This Act began a new chapter in British unemployment policy. It expanded the insurance scheme and laid down that the new scheme must remain financially solvent. The outstanding feature of the Act was the creation of the Unemployment Assistance Board to take control of unemployment payments and to have responsibility for the welfare of the unemployed. This was an entirely new departure in social legislation. The Board was to be an independent authority with its own staff and was designed to remove the care of the unemployed from the sphere of politics. The Act is extremely long and complicated and some of its main provisions are given in the following extract.

UNEMPLOYMENT INSURANCE ACT 1934
(Public General Acts 24 and 25 Geo 5 c 29)

An Act to amend the Unemployment Insurance Acts, 1920 and 1933, and to make further provision for the training and assistance of persons who are capable of, and available for, work but have no work or only part-time or intermittent work; . . .

Be it enacted . . .

Part I: Amendment of Unemployment Insurance Acts

Insured Persons
1. (1) The minimum age for entry into insurance . . . shall instead of being the age of sixteen years, be the age (not being less than fourteen years) when a person attains the age at which under the law for the time being in force his parents cease to be under an obligation to cause him to attend school unless there is some reasonable excuse.

* * *

Benefit
3. (1) An insured contributor who is between the ages of sixteen and sixty-five years and is unemployed shall . . . be entitled . . . to receive in a benefit year, benefit—

(a) in respect of periods not exceeding in the aggregate one hundred and fifty-six days; and

(b) if qualified for additional days under the provisions of the next following subsection, in respect of additional days of which the maximum number shall be computed in a manner provided by that subsection.

(2) The following provisions shall have effect with respect to additional days—

(a) an insured contributor shall be qualified for additional days if at the beginning of the benefit year five insurance years have elapsed since the beginning of the insurance year in which he first became such a contributor. . . .

(b) the maximum number of additional days in any benefit year shall be computed, in the case of an insured contributor qualified for such days, by allowing to him days at the rate of three for every five contributions paid in respect of him as an insured contributor in respect of the last five years, less one day for every five days in which benefit has been paid to him in respect of the benefit years which ended in the last five years. . . .

*　　*　　*

Instruction and Training

13. (1) Every education authority shall, as soon as may be after the commencement of this Part of this Act, submit to the Minister proposals for the provision of such course of instruction as may be necessary for persons in their area between the minimum age for entry into insurance and the age of eighteen years who are capable of and available for work but have no work or only part-time or intermittent work, and, if the Minister approves the proposals with or without modifications, the authority shall provide such courses in accordance therewith. . . .

(3) The Minister, subject to the approval of the Treasury, may provide training courses for persons who have attained the age of eighteen years and are capable of and available for work but have no work or only part-time or intermittent work.

(4) The Minister, subject to the approval of the Treasury, may defray the cost of authorised courses provided by him and contribute towards the cost of any other authorised courses. . . .

14. (1) If any person (whether an insured contributor or not) who is between the minimum age for entry into insurance and the age of eighteen years is capable of and available for work but has no work or only part-time or intermittent work, the

Minister may require his attendance . . . at any authorised course at which he can reasonably be expected to attend. . . .

* * *

Financial Provisions

17. (1) There shall be constituted a committee to be called 'the Unemployment Insurance Statutory Committee', to give advice and assistance to the Minister in connection with the discharge of his functions. . . .

(2) The Committee shall, not later than the end of February in every year, make a report to the Minister on the financial condition of the Unemployment Fund . . . and shall also make a report to the Minister . . . whenever they consider that the fund is or is likely to become, and is likely to continue to be, insufficient to discharge its liabilities. . . .

(3) If the Committee at any time report that the Unemployment Fund is or is likely to become, and is likely to continue to be, insufficient to discharge its liabilities, or is and is likely to continue to be more than reasonably sufficient to discharge its liabilities, the report shall contain—

(a) recommendations for . . . such amendments as in the opinion of the Committee are required in order to make the fund, as the case may be, sufficient or no more than reasonably sufficient to discharge its liabilities; and

(b) an estimate of the effect which the amendments recommended will have on the financial condition of the fund. . . .

18. (5) If at any time it appears to the Minister, after consultation with the Treasury, that the Unemployment Fund is, or will shortly become, insufficient to discharge its liabilities . . . there shall be advanced to the fund out of moneys provided by Parliament such sums as appear to the Treasury to be required to enable the fund to discharge its liabilities.

(6) Any sums advanced . . . together with interest thereon at such a rate as may be fixed by the Treasury, shall be charged on the Unemployment Fund and shall be repaid out of that fund to the Exchequer in such manner as the Treasury may direct. . . .

* * *

Part II

Unemployment Assistance

Constitution and Functions of Unemployment Assistance Board.

35. (1) For the purposes of this Part of this Act there shall be constituted a Board, to be called 'the Unemployment Assistance Board'. . . .

(2) The functions of the Board shall be the assistance of persons . . . who are in need of work and the promotion of their welfare and, in particular, the making of provision for the improvement and re-establishment of such persons with a view to their being in all respects fit for entry into or return to regular employment, and the grant and issue to such persons of unemployment allowances. . . .

(3) For the purpose of securing the advice and assistance of persons having local knowledge and experience in matters affecting the functions of the Board under this Part of the Act, the Board shall arrange for the estabishment of advisory committees throughout Great Britain to act for such areas as the Board thinks fit, and may pay to members of such committees such travelling and other allowances . . . as the Board . . . may determine.

(4) A report on the operation of this Part of this Act shall be made annually by the Board to the Minister who shall lay every such report before Parliament.

36. (1) . . . this Part of this Act applies to any person in whose case the following qualifications are fulfilled, that is to say—

(a) that he has attained the age of sixteen years and has not attained the age of sixty-five years; and

(b) that he is either—

(i) a person whose normal occupation is employment in respect of which contributions are payable under the Widows', Orphans' and Old Age Contributory Pensions Acts, 1925 to 1932; or

(ii) a person who, not having normally been engaged in any remunerative occupation since attaining the age of sixteen years, might reasonably have expected that his normal occupation would have been as aforesaid but for the industrial circumstances of the district in which he resides; and

(c) that he is capable of and available for work. . . .

37. In the exercise of the functions of the Unemployment Assistance Board . . . the Board . . . may—

(a) provide and maintain training courses for persons who

have attained the age of eighteen years and make contributions in respect of the cost of the provision and maintenance of such courses by the Minister or by any local authority or other body; and

(b) make provision for the continuance of the training and instruction afforded in connection with any such training course by entering into agreements with local authorities whereby persons . . . may, as part of such training and instruction, be employed for periods not exceeding three months upon work for the authority of such a character as to render them more fit for entry into or return to regular employment. . . .

Allowances and Training

38. (1) Subject to the provisions of this Act an allowance may be granted thereunder to any person to whom this Part of this Act applies, if he proves—

(a) that he is registered for employment in the presribed manner . . .

(b) that he has no work or only such part-time or intermittent work as not to enable him to earn sufficient for his needs; and

(c) that he is in need of an allowance.

(2) The amount of any allowance to be granted . . . to an applicant shall be determined by reference to his needs, including the needs of any members of the household of which he is a member who are dependent on or ordinarily supported by him. . . .

39. (1) All applications for allowances . . . shall be determined by officers of the Unemployment Assistance Board. . . .

*　　*　　*

Financial

44. (1) There shall . . . be established a fund which shall be called the Unemployment Assistance Fund and shall . . . be under the control and management of the Unemployment Assistance Board; and all sums received by the Board shall be paid into the fund. . . .

45. (1) There shall be paid to the Unemployment Assistance Board by the council of every county and county borough an annual contribution towards the expenses of the Board. . . .

46. (1) All expenses of the Unemployment Assistance Board
. . . shall be defrayed out of the Unemployment Assistance
Fund. . . .

SCHEDULES: SECOND SCHEDULE

Weekly Rates of Unemployment Benefit

	Rate of Benefit
Class of person to whom rate applies	

Persons of the age of twenty-one and upwards and
young men and young women who are in receipt of
an increase of Benefit in respect of dependants.

Men	17/–
Women	15/–

Persons who have attained the age of eighteen years
but are under the age of twenty-one years, not being
persons in receipt of an increase of benefit in respect of
dependants

Young Men	14/–
Young Women	12/–

Persons who have attained the age of seventeen years
but are under the age of eighteen years

Boys	9/–
Girls	7/6

Persons who are under the age of seventeen years

Boys	6/–
Girls	5/–

India

---

20. ANNOUNCEMENT OF GOVERNMENT POLICY ON INDIA 1917

The growing demand in India for a greater measure of self-government, and the great part played by Indians in the war effort of the British Empire made considerable changes in the government of India inevitable after the War. In August 1917 Edwin Montagu, the Secretary of State for India, made the following declaration on behalf of the British Government. It marks the beginning of an important step forward in Indian self-government. The Indian people were encouraged to look forward to achieving 'Dominion status' as enjoyed by Canada and Australia. Unfortunately, however, the concessions made by the British Government were to fall far short of what many Indians expected.

ANNOUNCEMENT OF GOVERNMENT POLICY ON INDIA

Made in the House of Commons by the Secretary of State for India (the Rt. Hon. E. S. Montagu) (20 August 1917)

(Parliamentary Debates, House of Commons, 1917 5th Series vol 97 cols 1695–1696)

The Government of India have for some time been urging that a statement should be made in regard to Indian policy. . . . The policy of His Majesty's Government, with which the Government of India are in complete accord, is that of the increasing association of Indians in every branch of the administration, and the gradual development of self-governing institutions, with a view to the progressive realisation of responsible government in India as an integral part of the British Empire. They have decided that substantial steps in this direction should be taken as soon as possible, and that it is of the highest importance, as a preliminary to considering what these steps should be, that there should be a free and informal exhange of opinion between those in authority at home and in India. His Majesty's Government have accordingly decided, with His Majesty's approval, that I should accept the Viceroy's invitation to proceed to India to discuss these matters with the Viceroy and the Government of India, to consider with the Viceroy the views of local governments, and to receive with him the suggestions of representative bodies and others.

I would add that progress in this policy can only be achieved by successive stages. The British Government and the Government of India, on whom the responsibility lies for the welfare and advancement of the Indian peoples, must be the judges of the time and measure of each advance, and they must be guided by the co-operation received from those upon whom new opportunities of service will thus be conferred, and by the extent to which it is found that confidence can be reposed in their sense of responsibility.

Ample opportunity will be afforded for public discussion of the proposals, which will be submitted in due course to Parliament.

21. JOINT REPORT ON INDIAN CONSTITUTIONAL REFORMS (MONTAGU-CHELMSFORD REPORT) 1918

After making the important announcement of Government policy on India in August 1917, Edwin Montagu, the Secretary of State for India, visited India to discuss with the Viceroy, Lord Chelmsford, the means of carrying it into effect. The result of their discussions was the Montagu-Chelmsford Report of May 1918. Many of the proposals of this Report were embodied in the Government of India Act 1919. The Report examines the situation in India and makes detailed proposals for Indian constitutional development. The conclusion of the Report is given here.

JOINT REPORT ON

INDIAN CONSTITUTIONAL REFORMS 1918

(*Joint Report on Indian Constitutional Reforms* Cmd 9109 1918 pp 277–282)

CONCLUSION

Conception of India's future

349. We may conveniently now gather up our proposals, so as to present a general picture of the progress which we intend and of the nature and order of the steps to be taken on the road. Our conception of the eventual future of India is a sisterhood of States, self-governing in all matters of purely local or provincial interest, in some case corresponding to existing provinces, in others perhaps modified in area according to the character and economic interests of their people. Over this congeries of States would preside a central Government, increasingly representative of and responsible to the people of all of them; dealing with matters, both internal and external, of common interest to the whole of India; acting as arbiter in inter-state relations, and representing the interests of all India on equal terms with the self-governing units of the British Empire. In this picture there is a place also for the Native States. It is possible that they too will wish to be associated for certain purposes with the organisation of British India, in such a way as to dedicate their peculiar qualities to the common service, without loss of individuality.

Changes in Control by the Government of India . . .

350. But it seems to us axiomatic that there cannot be a completely representative and responsible Government of India on an equal footing with the other self-governing units of the British Commonwealth until the component States whose people it represents and to whom it is responsible, or at least the great majority of them, have themselves reached the stage of full responsible government. Nor even then can we say that the form or the degree of responsibility which will be reached in India will exactly correspond to that attained by the Dominions. The final form of India's constitution must be evolved out of the conditions of India, and must be materially affected by the need for securing imperial responsibilities. The dominating factor in the intermediate process must be the rate at which the provinces can move towards responsible government. At the same time change obviously cannot be confined to the provinces. In proportion as they become more responsible the control which the Government of India exercises over them must diminish. But it is not merely a question of the extent of the control, the nature and manner of its exercise must in course of time be modified. We cannot think that States on the way to responsible government, which have imbibed a large element of responsibility into their constitutions, can be controlled by a purely autocratic power. So also with the duties extending over the whole of India which will be discharged by the Government of India as its special concern. It is impossible that while other duties which differ from them mainly in being local in scope or subject to provincial differentiation are being administered by responsible governments, those which fall to the Government of India should be administered autocratically. It follows, therefore, that change in the provinces implies change in the Government of India, but it does not imply that the change should be simultaneous or in equal proportion. On the contrary the change need simply be so much as to render the Government of India a suitable instrument for controlling the provinces at the stage at which they have for the time being arrived.

. . . and by the India Office . . .

351. Similarly all movement towards responsible government in India implies a corresponding change in the constitution of

the controlling agency in England. We cannot predict what kind of agency India will wish to maintain in London once she has attained the status of full partnership in the Empire; but it must be very different from the existing arrangements. These are based upon complete control by Parliament through the Secretary of State over every phase of administration in India. The Secretary of State is advised, and to some extent controlled, in the exercise of his functions by a Council designed to supply defects of direct knowledge and experience of India in himself and his subordinates in the India office: and also to watch the interests of India in cases where these may be threatened by competing British interests. Both Secretary of State and Council however, are in almost complete subordination to Parliament, which may, if it chooses, exercise its authority over every detail of administration in India. Now in relation to India Parliament will, we imagine, observe the principles long adopted towards the British self-governing colonies, and will contract its interference and control in direct proportion to the expansion of self-government. As this grows, the volume of business in which Parliament will interfere will steadily shrink, and the occasions will be rarer on which the Secretary of State will have to exercise control and will need to be advised regarding its exercise. This points to a diminution in the establishment of the India Office and possibly to a modification in the Council of India. But here, again, it is a question not merely of the volume of work but also of the spirit in which it is conducted. In dealing with organisations which have become largely representative and in some degree responsible, the need for mutual understanding and action strengthened by consent will be continually enhanced.

. . . and by Parliament . . .

352. Again, while the growth of responsibility in India will lead to decreased intervention by the Secretary of State and Parliament in day-to-day administration, the fact that India's further political progress is to be determined by Parliament makes it imperative that Parliament should be better informed about and more keenly interested in Indian conditions. The decisions to be taken in the future must to some extent be controversial; different advice about them will be offered from different

sources and Parliament, which is the final arbiter of India's destiny, should be in a position to form a wise and independent judgment. For these reasons we have suggested means of improving its opportunities of exercising a well-informed control.

Review of Proposals

353. We conclude therefore that change in any one portion of the Indian policy will involve changes on parallel lines but by no means at an equal pace in the other portions: and we claim that our proposals satisfy this fundamental principle. We begin with a great extension of local self-government so as to train the electorates in the matters which they will best understand. Simultaneously we provide for a substantial measure of self-government in the provinces and for better representation and more criticism in the Government of India and for fuller knowledge in Parliament. And we suggest machinery by means of which at regular stages the element of responsibility can be continuously enlarged and that of official control continuously diminished, in a way that will guarantee ordered progress and afford an answer to intermediate representations and agitation.

Need for criticism

354. In a matter of so great intricacy and importance it is obvious that full and public discussion is necessary. Pledges have been given that the opportunity for such discussion will be afforded. All that we ask therefore of His Majesty's Government for the present is that they will assent to the publication of our report. As we have said already, because it contemplates transitional arrangements, it is open to the criticisms which can always be effectively directed against all such plans. Hybrid executives, limited responsibility, Assemblies partly elected and partly nominated, divisions of functions, reservations general or particular, are devices that can have no permanent abiding place. They bear on their faces their transitional character; and they can be worked only if it is clearly recognised that that is their justification and their purpose. They cannot be so devised as to be logical. They must be charged with potentialities of friction. Hope of avoiding mischief lies in facing the fact that they are temporary expedients for training purposes, and in providing that the goal is not merely kept in sight but made attain-

able, not by agitation but by the operation of machinery inherent in the scheme itself. The principle laid down was the progressive realisation of responsible government. We have chosen the province as the unit in which it should be realised. Within that unit we intend, as far as is possible, immediate and complete responsibility in local affairs; responsibility within provincial governments in certain subjects, first to constituencies and then to the legislative councils; the reservation of other matters to a part of the executive Government whose responsibility to Parliament shall for the time being continue; a machinery for periodic inquiry with a view to the progressive diminution and eventual disappearance of the reserved subjects. We recommend no alteration at present in the responsibility of the Government of India to Parliament—except in so far as the transfer of subjects to popular control in the provinces *ipso facto* removes them from the purview of the Government of India and the Secretary of State—but we do provide greater opportunities for criticising and influencing the actions of the Government of India, and also a legislature which can develop when the day of responsibility comes into the machinery adapted to the new motive power. For these temporary purposes we have selected after a prolonged examination of alternatives what seemed to us the best transitional mechanism. Our proposals can only benefit by reasoned criticism both in England and India, official and non-official alike. They should be examined by the local Governments with whom we conferred but before whom we have not had an opportunity of placing them in their final form.

* * *

356. We have only one more word to say. If anything could enhance the sense of responsibility under which our recommendations are made in a matter fraught with consequences so immense, it would be the knowledge that even as we bring our report to an end far greater issues still hang in the balance upon the battlefields of France. It is there and not in Delhi or Whitehall that the ultimate decision of India's future will be taken. The liberty of the world must be won before our deliberations over the liberalising of Indian political institutions can acquire any tangible meaning. We cannot close this document more fittingly than with the prayer, which we know all India echoes,

that the principles of justice and freedom may be saved to the world by the splendid endurance and self-sacrifice of His Majesty's and the Allied armies.

EDWIN S. MONTAGU.   CHELMSFORD.

Simla;
22 April 1918

22. GOVERNMENT OF INDIA ACT 1919

This Act contained the main proposals of the Montagu-Chelmsford Report of 1918. It constituted a considerable advance in the development of self-government in India, though it failed to satisfy many Indians who demanded a more rapid advance. The Indian National Congress under its leader Gandhi agitated for a much greater degree of independence and self-government than that granted by the Act of 1919. Their agitation gained much support after the so-called 'massacre of Amritsar' of April 1919 when a large crowd of Indians who had assembled in defiance of a government order was fired upon by troops and 379 were killed. The new constitution embodied in the Act of 1919 therefore started in very difficult circumstances, and, not surprisingly, was never a complete success, though it remained in force until 1935. A selection of the main provisions of the Act is given below.

GOVERNMENT OF INDIA ACT 1919
(Public General Acts 8–10 Geo 5 c 101)

An Act to make further provision with respect to the Government of India. (23 December 1919)

WHEREAS it is the declared policy of Parliament to provide for the increasing association of Indians in every branch of Indian administration, and for the gradual development of self-governing institutions, with a view to the progressive realisation of responsible government in British India as an integral part of the empire:

And whereas progress in giving effect to this policy can only be achieved by successive stages, and it is expedient that substantial steps in this direction should now be taken:

And whereas the time and manner of each advance can be determined only by Parliament, upon whom responsibility lies for the welfare and advancement of the Indian peoples:

And whereas the action of Parliament in such matters must be guided by the co-operation received from those on whom new opportunities of service will be conferred, and by the extent to which it is found that confidence can be reposed in their sense of responsibility:

And whereas concurrently with the gradual development of

self-governing institutions in the Provinces of India it is expedient to give to those Provinces in provincial matters the largest measure of independence of the Government of India, which is compatible with the due discharge by the latter of its own responsibilities:

Be it therefore enacted . . . as follows:

Part I: Local Governments

1. (1) Provision may be made by rules under the Government of India Act 1915 . . . (referred to as the Principal Act)—

(a) for the classification of subjects, in relation to the functions of government, as central and provincial subjects, for the purpose of distinguishing the functions of local governments and local legislatures from the functions of the Governor-General in Council and the Indian legislature;

(b) for the devolution of authority in respect of provincial subjects to local governments, and for the allocation of revenues or other moneys to those governments;

(c) for the use under the authority of the Governor-General in Council of the agency of local governments in relation to central subjects, in so far as such agency may be found convenient, and for determining the financial conditions of such agency; and

(d) for the transfer from among the provincial subjects of subjects (in this Act referred to as 'transferred subjects') to the administration of the governor acting with ministers appointed under this Act, and for the allocation of revenue or moneys for the purpose of such administration

* * *

3. (1) The presidencies of Fort William in Bengal, Fort St George, and Bombay, and the provinces known as the United Provinces, the Punjab, Bihar and Orissa, the Central Provinces, and Assam, shall each be governed, in relation to reserved subjects (i.e. provincial subjects, other than transferred subjects), by a governor in council, and in relation to transferred subjects . . . by the governor acting with ministers appointed under this Act.

The said presidencies and provinces are in this Act referred to 'as governor's provinces' and the two first-named presidencies are in this Act referred to as the presidencies of Bengal and Madras.

4. (1) The governor of a governor's province may, by notification, appoint ministers, not being members of his executive council or other officials, to administer transferred subjects, and any ministers so appointed shall hold office during his pleasure.

There may be paid to any minister so appointed in any province the same salary as is payable to a member of the executive council in that province, unless a smaller salary is provided by a vote of the legislative council of the province.

(2) No minister shall hold office for a longer period than six months, unless he is or becomes an elected member of the local legislature.

(3) In relation to transferred subjects, the governor shall be guided by the advice of his ministers, unless he sees sufficient cause to dissent from their opinion, in which case he may require action to be taken otherwise than in accordance with that advice. Provided that rules may be made under the principal Act for the temporary administration of a transferred subject where, in cases of emergency, owing to a vacancy, there is no minister in charge of the subject, by such authority and in such manner as may be prescribed by the rules.

(4) The governor of a governor's province may at his discretion appoint from among the non-official members of the local legislature council secretaries, who shall hold office during his pleasure, and discharge such duties in assisting members of the executive council and ministers, as he may assign to them.

There shall be paid to council secretaries so appointed such salary as may be provided by vote of the legislative council.

A council secretary shall cease to hold office if he ceases for more than six months to be a member of the legislative council.

*   *   *

7. (1) There shall be a legislative council in every governor's province, which shall consist of the members of the executive council and of members nominated or elected as provided by this Act.

The governor shall not be a member of the legislative council, but shall have the right of addressing the council, and may for that purpose require the attendance of its members.

(2) The number of members of the governor's legislative councils shall be in accordance with the table set out in the First Schedule to this Act; and of the members of each council not more than twenty per cent be official members, and at least seventy per cent shall be elected members. . . .

10. (1) The local legislature of any province has power, subject to the provisions of this Act, to make laws for the peace and good government of the territories for the time being constituting that province.

(2) The local legislature of any province may, subject to the provisions of the subsection next following, repeal or alter as to that province any law made either before or after the commencement of this Act by any authority in British India other than that local legislature.

(3) The local legislature of any province may not, without the previous sanction of the Governor-General, make or take into consideration any law—

(a) imposing or authorising the imposition of any new tax . . .

(b) affecting the public debt of India, or the customs duties or any other tax or duty for the time being in force and imposed by the authority of the Governor-General in Council for the general purposes of the government of India . . .

(c) affecting the discipline or maintenance of any part of His Majesty's naval, military, or air forces . . .

(d) affecting the relations of the government with foreign princes or states; or

(e) regulating any central subject; or

(f) regulating any provincial subject which has been declared . . . to be either in whole or in part subject to legislation by the Indian Legislature, . . . or

(g) affecting any power expressly reserved to the Governor-General in Council by any law for the time being in force; or

(h) altering or repealing the provisions of any law which . . . is declared . . . to be a law which cannot be repealed or altered by the local legislature without previous sanction; or

(i) altering or repealing any provision of an Act of the Indian Legislature made after the commencement of this Act, which by the provisions of that Act may not be repealed or altered by the local legislature without previous sanction.

(4) The local legislature of any province has not power to make any law affecting any Act of Parliament.

* * *

11. (2) The estimated annual expenditure and revenue of the province shall be laid in the form of a statement before the [governor's legislative] council in each year, and the proposals of the local government for the appropriation of provincial revenues and other moneys in any year shall be submitted to the vote of the council in the form of demands for grants. The council may assent, or refuse its assent, to a demand, or may reduce the amount therein referred to either by a reduction of the whole grant or by the omission or reduction of any items of expenditure of which the grant is composed.

Provided that—

(a) the local government shall have power, in relation to any such demand, to act as if it had been assented to, notwithstanding the withholding of such assent or the reduction of the amount therein referred to, if the demand relates to a reserved subject, and the governor certifies that the expenditure provided for by the demand is essential to the discharge of his responsibility for the subject and

(b) the governor shall have power in cases of emergency to authorise such expenditure as may be in his opinion necessary for the safety or tranquillity of the province, or for the carrying on of any department; and

(c) no proposal for the appropriation of any such revenues or other moneys for any purpose shall be made except on the recommendation of the governor, communicated to the council.

(3) Nothing in the foregoing subsection shall require proposals to be submitted to the council relating to the following heads of expenditure

(i) contributions payable by the local government to the Governor-General in Council, and

(ii) interest and sinking fund charges on loans; and

(iii) expenditure of which the amount is prescribed by or under any law; and

(iv) salaries and pensions of persons appointed by or with the approval of His Majesty or by the Secretary of State in Council; and

(v) salaries of judges of the high court of the province and of the advocate-general. If any question arises whether any proposed appropriation of moneys does or does not relate to the above heads of expenditure, the decision of the governor shall be final.

(4) Where any Bill has been introduced or is proposed to be introduced, or any amendment to a Bill is moved or proposed to be moved, the governor may certify that the Bill or any clause of it or the amendment affects the safety or tranquillity of his province or any part of it or of another province, and may direct that no proceedings or no further proceedings shall be taken by the council in relation to the Bill, clause or amendment, and effect shall be given to any such direction.

* * *

(7) Subject to the rules and standing orders affecting the council, there shall be freedom of speech in the governor's legislative councils. No person shall be liable to any proceedings in any court by reason of his speech or vote in any such council, or by reason of anything contained in any official report of the proceedings of any such council.

* * *

Part II: Government of India

17. Subject to the provisions of this Act, the Indian legislature shall consist of the Governor-General and two chambers, namely, the Council of State and the Legislative Assembly.

Except as otherwise provided by or under this Act, a Bill shall not be deemed to have been passed by the Indian legislature unless it has been agreed to by both chambers . . .

18. (1) The Council of State shall consist of not more than sixty members . . . of whom not more than twenty shall be official members. . . .

19. (2) The total number of members of the Legislative Assembly shall be one hundred and forty. The number of non-elected members shall be forty, of whom twenty-six shall be official members. The number of elected members shall be one hundred. . . .

Part V: Statutory Commission

41. (1) At the expiration of ten years after the passing of this Act the Secretary of State, with the concurrence of both Houses of Parliament, shall submit for the approval of His Majesty the names of persons to act as a commission for the purposes of this section.

(2) The persons whose names are so submitted, if approved by His Majesty, shall be a commission for the purpose of inquiring into the working of the system of government, the growth of education, and the development of representative institutions, in British India, and matters connected therewith, and the commission shall report as to whether and to what extent it is desirable to establish the principle of responsible government, or to extend, modify or restrict the degree of responsible government then existing therein, including the question whether the establishment of second chambers of the local legislatures is or is not desirable.

(3) The commission shall also inquire into the report on any other matter affecting British India and the provinces, which may be referred to the commission by His Majesty.

FIRST SCHEDULE

Legislative Council	Number of Members
Madras	118
Bombay	111
Bengal	125
United Provinces	118
Punjab	83
Bihar and Orissa	98
Central Provinces	70
Assam	53

23. INDIAN STATUTORY COMMISSION (THE SIMON COMMISSION) 1930

The Government of India Act 1919 had provided that a Commission should be established after ten years to inquire into the working of the system of government in India and to make recommendations as to its development. During the 1920s national feeling in India grew very rapidly and the Indian National Congress, led by Gandhi, demanded national independence and supported this demand by civil disobedience. In these conditions the moderate advances towards self-government made by the Act of 1919 did not work well, and in 1927, two years before the appointed time, the British Government constituted the Indian Statutory Commission. This Commission was made up of members of both Houses of Parliament under the chairmanship of Sir John Simon. It contained members of all three British political parties, and one of its members was Clement Attlee who was to be Prime Minister of the Government which finally granted independence to India in 1947. The Commission was criticised in India because it did not include any Indian members. When the members of the Commission visited India they had great difficulty in obtaining co-operation in their inquiries, and whilst the Report was being prepared the Congress party engaged in a boycott of the central and provincial governments and began a campaign of civil disobedience and non-payment of taxes. In reply the British Government arrested many of the leaders of the Congress party, including Gandhi, and within nine months in 1930 more than 50,000 Indians had been convicted of offences of civil disobedience. It was against this background that the Simon Commission Report was published in 1930. The Report is a detailed survey of the government of India and of the working of the 1919 Act together with recommendations for the future. The concluding section of the Report is given here.

REPORT OF

THE INDIAN STATUTORY COMMISSION 1930

(Report of Indian Statutory Commission 1930 Cmd 3568–3569 pp 311–316)

Part XII: General Survey and Conclusion

362. We have now reached the end of our task. By the terms of our Warrant of Appointment, and by the provisions of the section on which it was based, we have been required to survey the working of the existing system of government in British India and to make recommendations for its amendment. In particular, we are directed to report 'as to whether and to what extent it is desirable to establish the principle of responsible government, or to extend, modify, or restrict the degree of responsible government' now existing. The previous parts of this volume give our detailed and considered answer to these questions. But we realise how difficult it is, in dealing with matters so various and complicated to present to those who may not be experts on the subject of the Indian constitution, a clear picture of the main constitutional results which would be achieved if our suggestions were incorporated into the existing system. We propose, therefore, in this final chapter to point out the more important of the changes which we recommend. What follows must not be treated as a summary of this volume, for not only is it impossible in a brief survey to cover all its contents, but a bald statement of conclusions would tend to mislead if it were not accompanied by a consideration of the arguments which have led us to reach them. We shall, therefore, add, at each point which we are going to mention, the necessary references to earlier portions of our Report.

The Scope of our Proposals

363. British India at present has a constitution, based for the most part on the Government of India Act, which includes

(1) a Central Executive—the Governor-General in Council; and a Central Legislature—the Council of State and Legislative Assembly; and

(2) nine Provincial Governments, each associated with a Provincial Council, and covering between them ninety-seven per cent of the whole area. The balance is represented by the North-West Frontier Province and other minor administrations. Our proposals touch every part of this constitution. We will venture to repeat words which we used in the first paragraph of our former volume, when we wrote that we were

entering upon our task 'upon the basis and assumption that the goal defined by Mr Montagu represents the accepted policy to be pursued, and that the only proposals worthy to be considered are proposals conceived in the spirit of the announcement of 20 August 1917 and inspired with the honest purpose of giving to it its due effect.' We have kept this principle steadily in mind throughout the whole of our deliberations, and our recommendations are based upon it.

Outline of Provincial Changes

364. In the provinces, the main consequences of adopting our proposals would be as follows:

The boundary now set up between departments of which Indian Ministers may take charge and departments from which they are excluded will be removed, and this dyarchy will terminate.

The conduct of provincial administration as a whole will rest with a provincial Cabinet, the members of which will be chosen by the Governor. These Ministers, whether elected members of the legislature or not, will have joint responsibility for action and policy. The constitution of the provincial Cabinet will be elastic and, where and when the Governor considers it necessary, it will contain an official element.

The powers of the Governor for certain essential purposes, such as the protection of minorities, and of the civil service, will be defined, and will be exercised within the limits and under the conditions we have described.

Full powers of intervention in the event of a breakdown will remain in the hands of the Governor, subject to the direction of the Governor-General.

The Provincial Legislatures will be based upon a widened franchise—the extension we propose would treble the electorate and would include the admission of a large number of women voters.

Certain important minorities will be adequately protected by the continuance of communal electorates unless and until agreement can be reached upon a better method.

The Depressed Classes will get representation by reservation of seats.

The Legislatures will be enlarged, and the constituencies reduced to a more manageable size. The Provincial Councils instead of being, as at present, purely legislative bodies, will acquire certain powers of recasting their own representative system, so that each province may advance to self-government on lines which are found to be best suited for its individual needs, subject always to securing that the vote of the majority shall not introduce constitutional changes which would prejudice minority rights.

The provinces will be provided with enlarged financial resources.

As for provincial areas, the question whether some redistribution is desirable will at once be taken up; such cases as those of Sind and Oriya-speaking peoples will be the first to be considered.

Burma, which is admittedly not a natural part of British India, will be separated forthwith. Provision must be made without delay for framing its future constitution.

The administered areas of the North-West Frontier Province will now receive an advance in constitutional status represented by the creation of a local legislature, with powers which we have described. Both it and Baluchistan will acquire the right to representation at the Centre.

The complicated and interlacing systems of administration of the Backward Tracts will be revised, and such parts of these as remain excluded areas will come under the charge of the central administration.

Modifications at the Centre

365. We now pass to the Centre. The Legislative Assembly, which should be called the 'Federal Assembly,' will be reconstituted on the basis of the representation of the Provinces and other areas in British India according to population. Members representing Governors' Provinces will be elected by the Provincial Councils by the method of proportional representation, which will ensure that members belonging to minority communities will be included in sufficient numbers in the Federal Assembly. Members will be returned from the North-West Frontier Province and other areas outside the Governor's Provinces by methods appropriate to each case. The official members of the Federal Assembly will consist of such members of

the Governor-General's assembly as sit in the Lower House, together with twelve other nominated officials.

The Council of State will continue with its existing functions as a body of elected and nominated members chosen in the same proportions as at present. Its members, who must have high qualifications, will, so far as they are elected, be chosen by indirect election carried out by provincial Second Chambers if such bodies are constituted, or, failing this, by the Provincial Councils.

The existing legislative and financial powers of the two Chambers of the Central Legislature will remain as at present, but the Federal Assembly will also have the special function of voting certain indirect taxes, collected by a central agency, the net proceeds of which will fall into a Provincial Fund for the purpose of being distributed amongst the different units represented in the Federal Assembly.

The Central Executive will continue to be the Governor-General in Council, but the Governor-General will henceforward be the authority who will select and appoint his Executive Councillors. Existing qualifications will remain, but will be laid down in statutory rules made under the new Government of India Act, so that when occasion arises to modify these conditions hereafter this may be done without passing a new Act of Parliament. But any modification in the statutory rules made for this purpose would require to be laid before both Houses of Parliament and the approval of both Houses expressed by resolution.

It is proposed that among the members of the Governor-General's Council should be one whose primary function it would be to lead the Federal Assembly. We have made other suggestions relating to the composition and character of the Governor-General's Council, and we propose that the Commander-in-Chief should no longer be a member of it, or of the Central Legislature.

The Army
366. We have suggested for consideration a method by which, if agreement could be reached, the obstacle which the composition and functions of the Army in India present to the more rapid development of responsible government might be removed through treating the defence of India as a matter

which should fall within the responsibilities of the Governor-General, advised by the Commander-in-Chief, as representing the Imperial authorities, instead of being part of the responsibilities of the Government of India in relation to the Central Legislature.

Civil Services, High Courts, India Office

367. As regards the Civil Services of India, the Security Services must continue to be recruited as All-India Services by the Secretary of State, and their existing rights must be maintained. These Security Services include the Indian Civil Service and the Indian Police Service. It is a matter for consideration whether the Irrigation Service and the Forest Service should not be similarly recruited. The privilege of premature retirement will be extended.

The rates of Indianisation laid down by the Lee Commission for the Security Services will be maintained.

In addition to the existing Public Service Commission, we intend that there should be established by Statute similar bodies covering the provincial and subordinate services in all the Provinces.

The High Courts will be centralised, and the expenses of the High Courts will become a central charge.

As regards the India Office, the Governor-General in Council will remain in constitutional theory under the superintendence, direction and control of the Secretary of State, and the extent to which this control is relaxed or falls into desuetude will depend upon future practice, and cannot be laid down in the Statute.

Apart from the Secretary of State's authority over the Governor-General in Council, he will exercise no control over Provincial Governments, save in so far as he does so in connection with the exercise of special powers vested in the Governor.

The functions and composition of the Council of India will be modified. Its size will be reduced, and the majority of its members should have the qualification of more recent Indian experience than is required at present. The council will exist primarily as an advisory body, but independent powers will continue for (1) the control of Service conditions, and (2) the control of non-votable Indian expenditure.

Indian States

368. Lastly, for the purpose of promoting the closer association with British India of the Indian States in matters of common concern for India as a whole, we propose that the new Act should provide that it shall be lawful for the Crown to create a Council for Greater India, containing both representatives of the States and members representing British India. This Council would have consultative and deliberative functions in regard to a scheduled list of 'matters of common concern', together with such other subjects of common concern as the Viceroy from time to time certifies as suitable for consideration by the Council. We refer to Part VII of this volume for a more detailed account of the machinery and methods which we contemplate, and we put forward the proposals as designed to make a beginning in the process which may lead to the Federation of Greater India.

Conclusion

369. In writing this Report we have made no allusion to the events of the last few months in India. In fact, the whole of our principal recommendations were arrived at and unanimously agreed upon before these events occurred. We have not altered a line of our Report on that account, for it is necessary to look beyond particular incidents and to take a longer view.

Our object throughout has been to bring to the notice of the British Parliament and the British people such information as we are able to supply about the general conditions of the problem which now awaits solution, together with our considered proposals. We hope, at the same time, that our Indian fellow-subjects, after doing us the courtesy of studying the Report as a whole (for isolated sentences may give to any reader a wrong impression), will find that what we have put forward has been written in a spirit of genuine sympathy.

No one of either race ought to be so foolish as to deny the greatness of the contribution which Britain has made to Indian progress. It is not racial prejudice, nor imperialistic ambition, nor commercial interest, which makes us say so plainly. It is a tremendous achievement to have brought to the Indian subcontinent and to have applied in practice the conceptions of impartial justice of the rule of law, of respect for equal civic rights without reference to class or creed, and of a disinterested and incorruptible civil service. These are essential elements in any state which is advancing towards well-ordered self-government. In his heart, even the bitterest critic of British administration in India knows that India has owed these things mainly to Britain. But, when all this is said, it still leaves out of account the condition essential to the peaceful advance of India, and Indian statesmanship has now a great part to play. Success can only be achieved by sustained goodwill and co-operation, both between the great religious communities of India which have so constantly been in conflict, and between India and Britain. For the future of India depends on the collaboration of East and West, and each has much to learn from the other.

We have grown to understand something of the ideals which are inspiring the Indian national movement, and no man who has taken part in working the representative institutions of Britain can fail to sympathise with the desire of others to secure for their own land a similar development. But a constitution is something more than a generalisation: it has to present a constructive scheme. We submit our Report in the hope that it may furnish materials and suggest a plan by means of which Indian constitutional reconstruction may be peacefully and surely promoted.

All of which we submit for Your Majesty's gracious consideration.

JOHN SIMON, *Chairman*
BURNHAM
STRATHCONA
EDWARD CADOGAN
VERNON HARTSHORN
G. R. LANE FOX
C. R. ATTLEE

S. F. STEWART,
Secretary. London, 27 May 1930

Ireland

24. THE GOVERNMENT OF IRELAND ACT 1920

This Act was intended to placate Irish opinion and to bring to an end the extremely difficult and confused situation existing in Ireland. The Act divided Ireland into two parts each with Home Rule on the lines previously proposed in 1912. The six counties of Ulster accepted this arrangement and became a separate state. The rest of Ireland rejected the terms of the Act and continued to fight for complete independence. The main points of the Act are given in the following extract.

THE GOVERNMENT OF IRELAND ACT 1920
(Public General Acts 10 and 11 Geo 5 c 67)
An Act to Provide for the Better Government of Ireland. (23 December 1920)

Be it enacted . . .
Establishment of Parliaments for Southern Ireland and Northern Ireland and a Council for Ireland.
1. (1) And after the appointed day there shall be established in Southern Ireland a Parliament to be called the Parliament of Southern Ireland consisting of His Majesty, the Senate of Southern Ireland, and the House of Commons of Southern Ireland, and there shall be established for Northern Ireland a Parliament to be called the Parliament of Northern Ireland consisting of His Majesty, the Senate of Northern Ireland, and the House of Commons of Northern Ireland.

(2) For the purposes of this Act, Northern Ireland shall consist of the parliamentary counties of Antrim, Armagh, Down, Fermanagh, Londonderry and Tyrone, and the parliamentary boroughs of Belfast and Londonderry, and Southern Ireland

shall consist of so much of Ireland as is not comprised within the said parliamentary counties and boroughs.

2. (1) With a view to the eventual establishment of a Parliament for the whole of Ireland, and to bringing about harmonious action between the parliaments and governments of Southern Ireland and Northern Ireland and to the promotion of mutual intercourse and uniformity in relation to matters affecting the whole of Ireland . . . there shall be constituted . . . a Council to be called the Council of Ireland.

(2) . . . the Council of Ireland shall consist of a person nominated by the Lord Lieutenant . . . who shall be President and forty other persons of whom seven shall be members of the Senate of Southern Ireland, thirteen shall be members of the House of Commons of Northern Ireland.

The members of the Council of Ireland shall be elected in each case by the members of that House of the Parliament of Southern Ireland or Northern Ireland of which they are members . . .

* * *

4. . . . the Parliament of Southern Ireland and the Parliament of Northern Ireland shall respectively have power to make laws for the peace, order, and good government of Southern Ireland and Northern Ireland with the following limitations . . .

(1) The Crown or the succession to the Crown, or a regency, or the property of the Crown. . . .

(2) The making of peace or war. . . .

(3) The navy, the army, the air force, the territorial force. . . .

(4) Treaties or any relations with foreign states. . . .

* * *

6. Neither the Parliament of Southern Ireland nor the Parliament of Northern Ireland shall have power to repeal or alter any provision of this Act. . . .

* * *

8. EXECUTIVE AUTHORITY

(1) The Executive power in Southern Ireland and in Northern Ireland shall continue vested in His Majesty the King,

and nothing in this Act shall affect the exercise of that power. . . .

* * *

19. Unless and until the Parliament of the United Kingdom otherwise determine . . . the number of members to be returned by the constituencies in Ireland, to serve in the Parliament of the United Kingdom shall be forty-six. . . .

* * *

75. Notwithstanding the establishment of the Parliaments of Southern Ireland and Northern Ireland . . . the supreme authority of the Parliament of the United Kingdom shall remain unaffected and undiminished over all persons, matters, and things in Ireland and every part thereof. . . .

25. IRISH FREE STATE (AGREEMENT) ACT 1922

In the autumn of 1921, after long bargaining, a settlement was finally reached between the British Government and the Irish representatives. The settlement was descibed as 'Articles of Agreement for a Treaty between Great Britain and Ireland'. It was approved by the British Parliament in December 1921 and, after fierce controversy, by the Dail in January 1922. The terms were then incorporated into an Act of Parliament and passed in March 1922. The settlement created the Irish Free State as an independent unit with a status in the British Empire like that of Canada.

IRISH FREE STATE (AGREEMENT ACT) 1922
(Public General Acts 12 Geo 5 c 4)

An Act to give the force of Law to certain Articles of Agreement for a Treaty between Great Britain and Ireland . . . (31 March 1922)

Be it enacted . . .

1. (1) The Articles of Agreement for a Treaty between Great Britain and Ireland set forth in the Schedule to this Act shall have the force of law as from the date of the passing of this Act.

SCHEDULE

Articles of Agreement for a Treaty between Great Britain and Ireland, dated 6 December 1921

1. Ireland shall have the same constitutional status in the Community of Nations known as the British Empire as the Dominion of Canada, the Commonwealth of Australia, the Dominion of New Zealand, and the Union of South Africa, with a Parliament having powers to make laws for the peace order and good government of Ireland and an Executive responsible to that Parliament, and shall be styled and known as the Irish Free State.

2. Subject to the provisions hereinafter set out the position of the Irish Free State in relation to the Imperial Parliament and Government and otherwise shall be that of the Dominion of

Canada, and the law, practice and constitutional usage governing the relationship of the Crown or the Representative of the Crown and of the Imperial Parliament to the Dominion of Canada shall govern their relationship to the Irish Free State.

3. The representative of the Crown in Ireland shall be appointed in like manner as the Governor-General of Canada, and in accordance with the practice observed in the making of such appointments.

4. The oath to be taken by Members of the Parliament of the Irish Free State shall be in the following form:

I,................. do solemnly swear true faith and allegiance to the constitution of the Irish Free State as by law established and that I will be faithful to H. M. King George V, of the common citizenship of Ireland with Great Britain and her adherence to and membership of the group of nations forming the British Commonwealth of Nations.

7. The Government of the Irish Free State shall afford to His Majesty's Imperial Forces:

(a) In time of peace such harbour and other facilities . . . as may from time to time be agreed . . . and

(b) In time of war or of strained relations with a Foreign Power such harbour and other facilities as the British Government may require. . . .

12. If . . . (within a month of the passing of this Act) . . . an address is presented to His Majesty by both Houses of the Parliament of Northern Ireland to that effect, the powers of the Parliament and Government of the Irish Free State shall no longer extend to Northern Ireland, and the provisions of the Government of Ireland Act 1920 (including those relating to the Council of Ireland) shall so far as they relate to Northern Ireland, continue to be of full force and effect, subject to the necessary modifications.

Provided that if such an address is so presented a Commission consisting of three persons, one to be appointed by the Government of the Irish Free State, one to be appointed by the Government of Northern Ireland and one who shall be Chairman to be appointed by the British Government shall determine in accordance with the wishes of the inhabitants, so far as may be compatible with economic and geographic conditions the boundaries between Northern Ireland and the rest of Ireland. . . .

16. Neither the Parliament of the Irish Free State nor the Parliament of Northern Ireland shall make any law so as either directly or indirectly to endow any religion or to prohibit or restrict the free exercise thereof or give any preference or impose any disability on account of religious belief or religious status or affect prejudicially the right of any child to attend a school receiving public money without attending the religious instruction at the school or make any discrimination as respects State aid between schools under the management of different religious denominations or divert from any religious denomination or any educational institution any of its property except for public utility purposes and on payment of compensation.

Political Controversies

26. THE END OF THE COALITION: BALDWIN'S SPEECH AT THE CARLTON CLUB, 19 OCTOBER 1922

In October 1922, Lloyd George was faced with a revolt of some of the Conservatives against the Coalition and its leaders. Austen Chamberlain, who was Chancellor of the Exchequer in the Coalition Government, summoned a meeting of the Conservative Members of Parliament at the Carlton Club on 19 October in an attempt to secure support for continuing the Coalition. At this meeting the following speech attacking Lloyd George and the Coalition was made by Stanley Baldwin, who was President of the Board of Trade. Bonar Law also spoke in favour of ending the Coalition. The views of Baldwin and Bonar Law were accepted by the majority of the Conservative members. The meeting decided by 187 votes to 87 that the Conservatives should fight the forthcoming election as an independent party. This not only brought about the fall of Lloyd George, who resigned that same afternoon, and was never again to hold office, but it also brought Baldwin to the forefront in the Conservative Party and in May 1923, when Bonar Law resigned, Baldwin became Prime Minister.

BALDWIN'S SPEECH AT
THE CARLTON CLUB, 19 OCTOBER 1922

(Text in G. M. Young—*Stanley Baldwin* pp 40–42 Rupert Hart-Davis, London 1952)

My Lords and gentlemen—Mr Chamberlain has called this meeting, as he has very clearly, and with his accustomed felicity of speech, told you, to put before you the views of the majority of the Unionist members of the Cabinet; and it is my duty at this moment to put before you, very briefly and very clearly, the views of the minority in the Cabinet—that is, of myself and of Sir Arthur Boscawen.

I have long been aware that there was a good deal of discomfort (let me leave it at that) in the ranks of the Tory Party, and when, a short time ago, a conference of the Unionist members of the Cabinet was held to consider the political situation, there were only two courses open before me—one, an easy one, to keep silent; the other, a very difficult one, to say what I felt. I will put my views to you as I put them to my colleagues.

I will preface this by making one remark. It seems to me, from what Mr Chamberlain has said, that it is a very easy thing to enter into a Coalition, but that, having entered into it, it must be permanent, because at any moment that you feel you ought to leave that Coalition, you open yourself to charges of having deserted, because you wished to escape the responsibility for the acts of that Coalition. I am quite sure, speaking for myself, I have no desire of that kind. If I stand as an Independent Conservative at the election, I shall make it perfectly clear to my constituents that I accept full responsibility for everything up to the moment when I had to separate myself from my colleagues. But, after all, the essence of coalition is voluntary association, and you cannot compel people to coalesce in any particular form; and it seems to me that a fatal mistake was made in agreeing to go to an election without consulting the party as to whether they were willing or not to continue the arrangement which they entered into in 1918.

As I am only going to speak for a very short time, I will not beat about the bush, but will come right to the root of the whole difficulty, which is the position of the Prime Minister. The Prime Minister was described this morning in *The Times*, in the words of a distinguished aristocrat, as a live wire. He was described to me, and to others, in more stately language, by the Lord Chancellor, as a dynamic force, and I accept those words. He is a dynamic force, and it is from that very fact that our troubles, in our opinion, arise. A dynamic force is a very terrible thing; it may crush you, but it is not necessarily right.

It is owing to that dynamic force, and that remarkable personality, that the Liberal Party, to which he formerly belonged, has been smashed to pieces; and it is my firm conviction that, in time, the same thing will happen to our party. I do not propose to elaborate, in an assembly like this, the dangers and perils of that happening. We have already seen, during our association with him in the last four years, a section of our party hopelessly alienated. I think that if the present association is continued, and if this meeting agrees that it should be continued, you will see some more breaking up, and I believe the process must go on inevitably until the old Conservative Party is smashed to atoms and lost in ruins.

I would like to give you just one illustration to show what I mean by the disintegrating influence of a dynamic force. Take Mr Chamberlain and myself. Mr Chamberlain's services to the State are infinitely greater than any that I have been able to render, but we are both men who are giving all we can give to the service of the State; we are both men who are, or who try to be, actuated by principle in our conduct; we are men who, I think, have exactly the same views on the political problems of the day; we are men who I believe—certainly on my side— have esteem and perhaps I may add affection for each other; but the result of this dynamic force is that we stand here, today, he prepared to go into the wilderness if he should be compelled to forsake the Prime Minister, and I am prepared to go into the wilderness if I should be compelled to stay with him. If that is the effect of that tremendous personality on two men occupying the position that we do, and related to each other politically in the way that Mr Chamberlain and I are, that process must go on throughout the party. It was for that reason that I took the stand I did, and put forward the views that I did. I do not know what the majority here or in the country may think about it. I said at the time what I thought was right, and I stick all through to what I believe to be right.

27. DIFFERING VIEWS ON THE FORMATION OF THE NATIONAL GOVERNMENT 1931

In August 1931 the Labour Government led by Ramsay Mac-Donald found itself confronted by a very difficult situation. It held power by a very small majority and was dependent upon Liberal support; it was faced by a rising tide of unemployment and by a financial crisis which seemed to be threatening British economic and financial stability. Parliament was in recess, but the Labour Cabinet Ministers returned to London. After long negotiations, and after attempts to find solutions to the problems facing the country which would be acceptable to the whole Cabinet had failed, the Labour Government resigned (24 August). Ramsay MacDonald then became Prime Minister of a National Government. His action aroused bitter controversy and most of his former colleagues in the Labour Party, led by Arthur Henderson, the former Foreign Secretary, refused to support him. The two extracts quoted here give some indication of the views expressed at the time.

(27a) The Times 25 August 1931

The country awakens this morning to find Mr MacDonald still Prime Minister, with the prospect of a small Cabinet representative of all three parties. The former Cabinet resigned yesterday afternoon, and a statement issued last night announced that considerable progress had been made towards settling the composition of its successor, which would be a Government of co-operation formed for the specific purposes only of carrying through a very large reduction of expenditure and raising 'on an equitable basis' of the further funds required to balance the Budget. On Sunday night it had already become clear that the courageous determination of Mr MacDonald and Mr Snowden to adopt a policy of retrenchment, including especially cuts in the dole, had cleft an unbridgeable gulf between two sections in the Socialist Cabinet; but it was not until yesterday morning that a salutary and steadying announcement from Buckingham Palace revealed that the leaders of all three parties, having been summoned to visit the King, were considering the formation of a National Government.

All concerned are to be warmly congratulated on this result, so fully in accord with the patriotic spirit which has inspired a week's most anxious negotiations. The PRIME MINISTER and the colleagues of his own party who have followed him deserve in particular unqualified credit, both for the manner in which they took their political lives in their hands by facing and forcing the break-up of the late Cabinet, and for their new decision to translate courage in the Cabinet into courage in the country. Their readiness to share the responsibility—honour is perhaps the better word—of carrying through to the end a policy of retrenchment adds enormously to the prospect of its success. No one henceforth will ever be able to claim that retrenchment is a class or partisan policy, dictated solely by an unsubstantial panic manufactured by industrial and financial interests. No Conservative or Liberal—it may be earnestly hoped— will deny his share in an arrangement to carry out that part of a national task which all are agreed must come first and cannot be delayed. A General Election has been averted. That in itself is a great thing gained, for a General Election now would have been disastrous, whatever its result. Decision would have been postponed at a moment when speed is by far the most important element in the value of decision. The country would have been for weeks without an effective Government at a time when it never needed more to be governed. As it is, the King's Government will be carried on with all the materials available for moving surely and swiftly. And for this boon, be it said, the public has no one to thank more sincerely than the King himself. His Majesty's prompt return to London on Sunday morning was a wise inspiration. He has, of course, left wholly to his Ministers the business of moulding policy and of trying to settle their differences. But he was able to bring the leaders together as no one else could have done so well, and by delaying the Prime Minister's resignation he did much to substitute a constructive effort for a tired man's impulse of despair. In a strictly constitutional capacity he has rendered a signal service to his people.

It is an interesting, dramatic, and logical fact that the Labour Government has fallen in what has always been foreseen to be the acid test of democracy—namely, the capacity of its leaders to tell the people the truth and not to regulate their policy by the votes that it would bring. That is the test which Mr Mac-

Donald, Mr Snowden, and those who supported them have triumphantly survived. That is the test to which their dissentient colleagues have ingloriously succumbed. . . . The measure of their ignominy is their experience of practical affairs and their weight in the party counsels, and, judged by this criterion, Mr Henderson has achieved a miserable pre-eminence. He may indeed be accounted the ringleader of the rebels; and yet as Foreign Secretary, as a former member of a National Government, and as party manager, he had more reason than most of them to know how real is the present danger, what course experience dictated, and how a powerful influence in favour of that course could best be exercised. He has chosen to aim at the leadership of folly rather than to preserve the loyalty of a follower of wisdom. Though he looked, at one time—perhaps by good fortune—as though he might emerge from this Parliament with more credit than some of his colleagues, his Foreign Secretaryship is likely now to be remembered only for its final indifference to the position of his country in the world.

(27b) New Statesman 29 August 1931

In many respects the situation which confronted the Cabinet was like that of August 1914. . . . In 1914 Mr MacDonald refused to join a War Cabinet: Mr Henderson accepted. Mr MacDonald was denounced as a traitor: Mr Henderson applauded. In leading articles in The Times, for instance, Mr MacDonald's patriotism is extolled, while Mr Henderson is denounced as a man who put party before country. Meanwhile, in Labour circles all over the country Mr MacDonald is being denounced—against Mr Henderson's expressed wish—for betraying his party. Neither denunciation of Mr MacDonald nor of Mr Henderson is just.

Mr MacDonald's decision to form a Cabinet in conjunction with the Liberals and Tories seems to us a mistake, just as it would have been a mistake for him as a pacifist to join a War Cabinet in 1914. For he must inevitably find himself at war with the whole of organised labour, and not only with organised labour, but with all those, in all classes, who believe that the policy of reducing the purchasing power of the consumer to meet a situation of over-production is silly economics. . . . An effort is being made to represent the issue as merely one of a 10 per cent reduction in the dole, as if patriotism meant cutting the dole and refusal to cut it could only be based on cowardly subservience to the electorate. . . . We oppose it . . . because it is only a first step, the crucial beginning of a policy of reductions, disastrous, we believe, alike for England and the rest of the world. . . .

On the personal side we may respect Mr MacDonald's position. He has nothing to make out of it: he goes and goes consciously away from his party. He must find himself out of sympathy with the majority of his colleagues in the new Cabinet, and he will not find it easy to dissociate himself from their views on many subjects. . . . *The Times* will easily co-operate in doing the unpopular, dirty work—in cutting the dole, forcing down wages and cutting education and the social services. In doing so they will probably increase unemployment, and the various remedies for unemployment must speedily come up for discussion. The Tory remedy is tariffs, and in the depth of depression to which the policy of deflation will soon have reduced the country, a very popular policy it will be. . . . But where will the Liberals be, and where Mr MacDonald? . . . The Tories played their cards well; the Labour Party may be grateful to Mr Henderson for saving it from disruption and discredit.

Commonwealth

28. THE BRITISH COMMONWEALTH OF NATIONS

The new status of the Dominions was recognised at the end of the First World War by the fact that they were represented at the Peace Conference, and that the treaties were signed not only by the British but also by the Dominion Ministers of the Crown. They were also recognised in the League of Nations.

At the Imperial Conference of 1926 a Committee was appointed under the chairmanship of Lord Balfour to inquire into and to define the relationship between Great Britain and the Dominions. The Report of the Inter-Imperial Relations Committee was accepted by the Conference and was given legal effect by the Statute of Westminster, 1931.

The Statute had been debated in the Parliaments of the Dominions and was then presented to the British Parliament to be enacted. It formally recognised the freedom which the Dominions already possessed, and it acknowledged that common allegiance to the Crown was the only link which united the various members of the Commonwealth. The Statute of Westminster completed the process whereby the British Empire was transformed into a Commonwealth of independent states co-operating together in freedom and without restraint of any kind.

(28a) Extract from the Report of Inter-Imperial Relations Committee 1926
Parliamentary Papers 1926 *Cmd 2768*

Status of Great Britain and the Dominions

The Committee are of opinion that nothing would be gained by attempting to lay down a Constitution for the British Empire. Its widely scattered parts have very different characteristics, very different histories, and are at very different stages of evolution; while, considered as a whole, it defies classification and bears no real resemblance to any other political organisation which now exists or has ever yet been tried.

There is, however, one most important element in it which, from a strictly constitutional point of view, has now, as regards all vital matters, reached its full development—we refer to the group of self-governing communities composed of Great Britain and the Dominions. Their position and mutual relation may be readily defined. *They are autonomous communities within the British Empire, equal in status, in no way subordinate to one another in any aspect of their domestic or external affairs, though united by a common allegiance to the Crown, and freely associated as members of the British Commonwealth of Nations.*

(*28b*) *The Statute of Westminster 1931* (*Public General Acts 22 Geo 5 c 4*)

An Act to give effect to certain resolutions passed by Imperial Conferences held in the years 1926 and 1930 (11 December 1931)

Whereas the delegates of His Majesty's Governments in the United Kingdom, the Dominion of Canada, the Commonwealth of Australia, the Dominion of New Zealand, the Union of South Africa, the Irish Free State and Newfoundland, at Imperial Conferences holden at Westminster in the years of our Lord nineteen hundred and twenty-six and nineteen hundred and thirty did concur in making the declarations and resolutions set forth in the Reports of the said Conferences:

And whereas it is meet and proper to set out by way of preamble to this Act that, inasmuch as the Crown is the symbol of the free association of the members of the British Commonwealth of Nations, and as they are united by a common allegiance to the Crown, it would be in accord with the established constitutional position of all the members of the Commonwealth in relation to one another that any alteration in the law touching the Succession to the Throne or the Royal Style and Titles shall hereafter require the assent as well of the Parliaments of all the Dominions as of the Parliament of the United Kingdom:

And whereas it is in accord with the established constitutional position that no law hereafter made by the Parliament of the United Kingdom shall extend to any of the said Dominions as part of the law of that Dominion otherwise than at the request and with the consent of that Dominion:

And whereas it is necessary for the ratifying, confirming and establishing of certain of the said declarations and resolutions of the said Conferences that a law is made and enacted in due form by authority of the Parliament of the United Kingdom:

And whereas the Dominion of Canada, the Commonwealth of Australia, the Dominion of New Zealand, the Union of South Africa, the Irish Free State and Newfoundland have severally requested and consented to the submission of a measure to the Parliament of the United Kingdom for making such provision with regard to the matters aforesaid as is hereinafter in this Act contained:

Now, therefore, be it enacted . . . as follows:

1. In this Act the expression 'Dominion' means any of the following Dominions, that is to say, the Dominion of Canada, the Commonwealth of Australia, the Dominion of New Zealand, the Union of South Africa, the Irish Free State and Newfoundland.

2. . . . . No law and no provision of any law made after the commencement of this Act by the Parliament of a Dominion shall be void or inoperative on the ground that it is repugnant to the law of England. . . .

3. It is hereby declared and enacted that the Parliament of a Dominion has full power to make laws having extra-territorial operation.

4. No Act of Parliament of the United Kingdom passed after the commencement of this Act shall extend, or be deemed to extend, to a Dominion as part of the law of that Dominion, unless it is expressly declared in that Act that the Dominion has requested, and consented to, the enactment thereof.

International Disputes

29. THE ABYSSINIAN CRISIS 1935

During 1935 it became more and more apparent that Mussolini was preparing for an attack upon Abyssinia. As early as 3 January 1935 Abyssinia had appealed to the League of Nations against the threat of war from Italy. Action was postponed by Italian promises to negotiate, but meanwhile Italy continued throughout the spring and summer to prepare for war.

It was clear that this was going to be a crucial test of the strength of the League of Nations, and it was against this background that the British Foreign Secretary, Sir Samuel Hoare, visited Geneva to address the Assembly of the League on 11 September 1935. His speech calling for support for the League made a great impression upon the Assembly and was received with enthusiasm, but did not prevent the invasion of Abyssinia by Italy on 3 October 1935.

(*29a*) *Extract from a speech by Sir Samuel Hoare* (*British Secretary of State for Foreign Affairs*) *to the assembly of the League of Nations at Geneva 11 September 1935*
(*From* The Times *12 September 1935*)

... I do not suppose that in the history of the Assembly there was ever a more difficult moment for a speech and a discussion. When the world is stirred to excitement over the Abyssinian controversy and feeling runs high upon one side or the other ... I will begin by reaffirming the support of the League by the Government that I represent, and the interest of the British people in collective security. ...

The League is what its member-States make it. If it succeeds it is because its members have in combination with each other, the will and the power to apply the principles of the Covenant. If it fails, it is because its members lack either the will or the power to fulfil their obligations. ...

If the burden is to be borne, it must be borne collectively. If risks for peace are to be run, they must be run by all. The security of the many cannot be ensured solely by the efforts of a few, however powerful they may be. On behalf of his Majesty's Government in the United Kingdom I can say that they will be second to none in their intention to fulfil, within the measure of their capacity, the obligations which the Covenant lays upon them.

... In conformity with its precise and explicit obligations, the League stands, and my country stands with it, for the collective maintenance of the Covenant in its entirety, and particularly to all acts of unprovoked aggression. The attitude of the British nation in the past few weeks has clearly demonstrated the fact that this is no variable and unreliable sentiment, but a principle of international conduct to which they and their Government hold with firm, enduring and universal persistence. . . .

The Debate in the Labour Party over the Abyssinian Crisis: The crisis over Italy's designs on Abyssinia created a very difficult problem for the Labour Party at its Annual Conference held at Brighton in 1935. The matter was debated on 1 October. If Italy did invade Abyssinia, the Party had to decide whether it would support the Government in any measures it took to uphold the League of Nations, either by economic sanctions against Italy or by direct military action. The problem was made very difficult because there were in the Labour Party a number of people who were opposed to the use of force in any circumstances, and who feared that economic sanctions against Italy would be only the first step towards another World War. Among those who felt in this way was George Lansbury, now 76 years of age, and the most loved and revered figure in the Labour Party. Since 1931 he had been leader of the Party. His point of view was opposed in a remarkable speech by Ernest Bevin, the representative of the Transport and General Workers' Union. The Trades Union Congress, meeting at Margate on 2 September 1935, had already condemned Italy's preparations for an attack on Abyssinia and had agreed by a large majority to support the Government and the League of Nations in any action to safeguard the independence of Abyssinia.

The debate at Brighton was of great importance for the future of the Labour Party. Very strong feelings were roused by the issue and were expressed in the many speeches which were made. The result was a crushing defeat for the pacifists in the Party. George Lansbury resigned the leadership shortly afterwards, and was succeeded by Clement Attlee. Extracts from the two main speeches are given below.

(*29b*) *Tuesday, October 1 Italy and Abyssinia Extract from the Debate on Sanctions against Italy at the Labour Party Conference held at Brighton, 1 October 1935*
(*From* Report of the 35th Annual Conference of the Labour Party 1935 *pp 153–180*)

The Chairman said that they were to begin their proceedings on what was possibly the biggest discussion, and one of the vastest importance, that the Conference had ever had to deal with, and, in order that the Conference might know precisely upon what it was to base its decision, he proposed to read the resolution that would be moved by Dr Hugh Dalton on behalf of the National Executive Committee.

Dr Hugh Dalton (National Executive) moved the following resolution:

This Conference, in full accord with the views expressed by organised Labour wherever freedom of expression exists, is gravely disturbed by the violation of the law of nations threatened by Italy under Fascist domination in preparing a war of conquest upon Abyssinia. The Conference declares its profound conviction that such violation of the sanctity of international treaties is destructive of the foundations of civilisation.

It condemns in the strongest terms the provocative and defiant attitude of the Head of the Italian Government towards the League of Nations. It appeals to the Italian people to honour their pledges to abandon War as an instrument of policy and their acceptance of responsibility jointly with all other members of the League for the maintenance of Peace.

United and determined in its opposition to the policy of imperialist aggression, this Conference calls upon the British Government, in co-operation with other nations represented at the Council and Assembly of the League, to use all the necessary measures provided by the Covenant to prevent Italy's unjust and rapacious attack upon the territory of a fellow member of the League. The Conference pledges its firm support of any action consistent with the principles and statutes of the League to restrain the Italian Government and to uphold the authority of the League in enforcing Peace.

While resolute in refusing to countenance any resort to War in flagrant violation of international treaties, or to permit Italy to profit by any act of aggression, this Conference recognises the imperative necessity of eradicating the evils and dangers arising from the economic exploitation of colonial territories and peoples for the profit of imperialist and capitalist powers and groups.

We therefore call upon the British Government to urge the League of Nations to summon a World Economic Conference, and to place upon its Agenda the international control of the sources and supply of raw materials, with the application of the principle of economic equality of opportunity for all nations in the undeveloped regions of the earth.

Rt. Hon. George Lansbury, M.P., who was received with loud and prolonged applause, said . . . I am in a very difficult position today. Often—and only the Executive and my colleagues know how often—I have disagreed with their policy, and because I was a member of the Executive, and lately because of my other position, I have remained silent during the whole of the Conference. I think last year I did not speak at all except to answer a question. I say that because I want everyone to understand that it is difficult for me to stand here today and publicly repudiate a big fundamental piece of policy. If I were in any doubt about that policy, I am sure I should not take the line I am taking, but I ask the Conference to believe me when I say that I have never been more convinced that I am right, and that the Movement is making a terrible mistake, than I am today. My only difficulty, and it is a real one, is my relationships with the Party. I agree with those of my friends—I know they will allow me still to say that, because we are all real friends in this matter—I agree with the position of those of my friends who think that it is quite intolerable that you should have a man speaking as Leader who disagrees fundamentally on an issue of this kind; and so, next Tuesday, in London, the Parliamentary Party (being the part of the Movement that elects the Leader) is meeting, and together we will discuss this matter, and I hope we shall arrive at a satisfactory solution. The Conference constitutionally is unable to deal with the matter, except by some kind of emergency motion of recommendation to the Parliamentary Party, or expressing its opinion on the situation. And I want to say that I should not consider an expression of opinion hostile to my continuance as Leader as anything more than natural and perfectly friendly. I hope that that statement will make it absolutely clear where I stand, because I am torn just like that.

*   *   *

But there is one thing that brings me to this microphone today and that is an overwhelming conviction, since I was a boy, that force is no remedy. During the last six years—first in the Labour Government, and secondly as Leader of the Party—I have been in a kind of Dr Jekyll and Mr Hyde position. I have had to speak for the Party, I have had to see Sir Samuel Hoare for the Party, and on each occasion when I have spoken for the Party and when I saw Sir Samuel Hoare, I tried honestly and straightforwardly to state the Party's position. If there be any inconsistency in that, well and good, I shall leave it at that. . . . I believe that force never has and never will bring permanent peace and permanent goodwill in the world. I believe also that we in our Movement have really said that, in dealing with our own striving for Socialism. We have said to the workers: 'We are sorry for your plight, but you must wait until you have converted the rest of the people to your point of view'. I have gone into mining areas, I have gone into my own district when people have been starving or semi-starving; I have stood in the midst of dockers who have been on the verge of starvation (before there was any 'dole' or Poor Law Assistance, excepting the workhouse), and I have said to them: 'No, you must not rise, you must have no violence, you must trust to the winning of this through public opinion.' I have never at any time said to the workers of this country: 'You must take up either arms, or sticks, or stones, in order to force your way to the end that you seek to attain.' And when I am challenged on all these issues I say to myself this: I have no right to preach pacifism to starving people in this country and preach something else in relation to people elsewhere. And that has been a fundamental state, it has not been something of expediency. It has been a belief that we should sooner or later in the world win our way with waiting. I have said the same thing on the continent when I have had the privilege of speaking abroad. I have said it in Russia when my Russian comrades allowed me to see a review of their air force, and when they took me on one of their warships. I have never under any circumstances said that I believe you could obtain Socialism by force.

And why have I said that? I have said it, first, because One Whose life I revere and Who, I believe, is the greatest Figure in history, has put it on record: 'Those who take the sword shall perish by the sword.' All history right down the ages proves that. You may go through the continent of America, and they have a problem on their hands just now which is insoluble in regard to Negroes; you may go to India, and you will see millions there living under terrible conditions. You may go into our own country and on the continent of Europe, and it is still a seething mass of discontent, a seething mass of unrest.

Perhaps you will say to me—it has been said—'But things are different now; the world has changed.' I would die a very happy man indeed, if I thought Europe and Britain and the world had been improved by the Great War. Someone said this afternoon something about armaments. Do you know that what terrified me in all this business was, we were told that the Germans were little by little rearming. We were told, somewhere about eighteen months ago, I think, that the Government had known that they were rearming. Then a panic seized the House of Commons, and increased armaments were demanded. Today there are more armaments in Europe, and very soon there will be much more armaments in this country than there was before the war. I would like to ask whoever replies to me: Is the increase in armaments a sign of collective security? Do we believe that each country has to pile up more and more armaments in order that we may all be secure? What a world! And it is not only Hitler, not only Mussolini, but at the other end of the world there is Japan, all of them feverishly rearming. And we met that, as we met it before 1914, by saying we must rebuild the British navy; if necessary, obtain a £200,000,000 loan; we must have the greatest air force that it is possible to create; we must mechanise our land forces, and we must in every possible way prepare our island for peace. For peace and mind you, we are going to move some of our schools from the south coast somewhere inland. No decision has been come to yet, but we are thinking of moving Woolwich Arsenal down into Wales. We are training our children for air drill and gas attack drill. There are pictures in the papers telling us all that. One newspaper comes out demanding that we should have conscription now. You have to ask yourselves what is all this for? Certainly not for Italy and Abysinnia. No one believes that. It was all started before this crisis became as acute as it is today.

We were told that the only means of defence against air attacks—this was not a statement made by a pacifist, but by a leading member of the present Government—is that we should massacre more women and children than those who might attack us. War becomes more bestial, more sickening every day. Christ said that we had to love one another. I try to, and I daresay most of you do. I cannot believe that the Christ whom you worship, or the saints whose memory you all adore, that for any reason or any cause, they would be found pouring bombs and poison gas on women and children or men for any reason whatsoever. Not even in retaliation because also it is written 'Vengeance is mine, I will repay.'

In 1919 the victorious nations told their people that they would give them vengeance on the Germans, that militarism was smashed, and it would never be rehabilitated. Today we know that that is not true. And now we are asked to put our faith in the same means through the League of Nations. I personally cannot see the difference between mass murder organised by the League of Nations, or mass murder organised between individual nations; to me it is exactly the same. I have spoken for Socialism on many an occasion, and the stock argument against me by Christians and Jews and people of all religious faiths, and of no religious faiths, has been, 'Oh, Socialism, it is a fine ideal, my boy, but you have got to change human nature first.' Well, I have never succumbed to that about Socialism, and I am not going to succumb to it about war.

I asked in Parliament—and Attlee has done it ably and consistently, and so have other of our members—this Government during the last four years to turn their minds away from war preparations, to turn their minds away from discussing the size of guns or the strength of poison gas, and to devote their energies to finding out how we could remove the causes of war. That is our stock argument about wrongs in our own country. Remove the causes that create the depressed areas, remove the causes that create unemployment. We have tried to get that dealt with by the Government of the day. Sir Samuel Hoare put his finger on what he thought was the spot of weakness in our case when he spoke at Geneva. He said that he was not sure that it was so much a difficulty of getting raw materials as it was of finding markets after you had worked out your raw materials. I am not quoting his exact words, but that is in effect what he meant and said.

I think that we in this Party have got to get down to that question, and to get down to it instead of backing this policy of sanctions. I was asked the other day what would I do if I went to Geneva. Well, first of all you have to get a mandate for what you want done, and it is a little unfair to say to a man like myself, How would you deal with the enormous problem now? But I will tell you, broadly, what I would do if I had the power to go to Geneva backed by our people, or if I went to a Conference of Labour backed by our people. I would go to them and say very much what Dr Salter said a little while ago, and that is that Great Britain—the great imperialist race—led by the common people of our race were finished with imperialism, that we were willing that all the peoples under our flag, wherever you can establish Government, should be free to establish their own Governments, that there should be no such thing as domination either in our lives or in our actions, but that we would be willing that the whole of the resources which are under our control should be pooled for the service of all mankind. Not handed out here and there to individual nations to exploit, but put under the positive control of an International Commission, and I would say, further, that I wanted our nation to say at the same time, because we wanted nothing from the other people but what we could give something fairly and squarely in exchange for, that we would be willing to become disarmed unilaterally.

I believe that the first nation that will put into practice practical Christianity, doing to others as you would be done unto, that that nation would lead the world away from war and absolutely to peace. And when I am asked, Would the nation ever agree to pay that price? I maintain what John Bright maintained—that if you put against the gains from imperialism the cost of those gains in human life and in values of all descriptions, that you are losers all the time; that there is no real gain for the toiling masses of the world; and that this Christianity, with its psalm singing and prayers—this Christianity is the realist principle of life, because it says 'We are willing that you shall carry out the doctrine of those who are strongest, helping with the strength of their brain and their power the weak.' I know that you will say to me: 'Say that to Mussolini, or say that to Hitler.' If I had had power during this period I would have gone and faced these men at Geneva and I would have let the world know what it was I was proposing to do.

This is no mere ideal; it is no greater international ideal than the national ideal of common service for each other within our own nation. We have got somewhere and at some time to begin, and I want our people to begin. And that is the message that somehow I must put to the world wherever people will hear me.

It may be that I shall not meet you on this platform any more. (Cries of 'No'.) There are things that come into life that make changes inevitable. It may very well be that in the carrying out of your policy I shall be in your way. When I was sick and on my back ideas came into my head, and one was that the only thing worth while for old men to do is to at least say the thing they believe, and to at least try to warn the young of the dangers of force and compulsion. Attlee says we have the compulsion of the police and of the law. Some day even that will pass away, when justice between man and man comes into being.

It is said that people like me are irresponsible. I am no more irresponsible a leader than the greatest Trade Union leader in the country. I live my life, as they do, amongst ordinary people. I see them when I am at home every day: I meet them and know all there is to know about them; and they do about me. But one thing I know is, that during the last war the youth, the early manhood of my division was slaughtered most terribly, and now I see the whole world rushing to perdition. I see us, as someone has said, rattling into barbarism again. If mine was the only voice in this Conference, I would say in the name of the faith I hold, the belief I have that God intended us to live peaceably and quietly with one another, if some people do not allow us to do so, I am ready to stand as the early Christians did, and say, 'This is our faith, this is where we stand, and, if necessary, this is where we will die.'

Mr Ernest Bevin (Transport and General Workers' Union) said: I want you this afternoon to be a little patient with me if I am somewhat tedious in dealing both with the background and the present position that the Trades Union Congress finds itself in. I think what I will say today my colleagues of the trades Union Congress will agree with, although they have not asked me to speak for them, but I happen to be their representative on the National Council of Labour, and we have had to take some responsibility, together with the Labour Party and the Parliamentary Executive, in shaping this policy and, having had to take some responsibility, we have now to give effect to it.

I think the Movement ought to understand the Trades Union Congress position. Let us remind the delegates that, when George Lansbury says what he has said today in the Conference, it is rather late to say it, and I hope this Conference will not be influenced by either sentiment or personal attachment. I hope you will carry no resolution of an emergency character telling a man with a conscience like Lansbury what he ought to do. If he finds that he ought to take a certain course, then his conscience should direct him as to the course he should take. It is placing the Executive and the Movement in an absolutely wrong position to be taking your conscience round from body to body asking to be told what you ought to do with it. There is one quotation from the Scriptures which George Lansbury has quoted today which I think he ought to apply to himself—'Do unto others.' I have had to sit in Conference with the Leader and come to decisions, and I am a democrat and I feel we have been betrayed.

It is all very well to cheer somebody you like and interrupt somebody you do not like, but I ask you to hear the arguments. The responsibility of some of us, representing, as I do personally, nearly half-a-million men in this Movement, is no light responsibility at all. 'Do unto others as you would they should do unto you,' he said. I wish that had been applied by him to the rest of the members of the National Joint Council, because at Margate, instead of coming back to say that he was in difficulties, he goes to the Press Association on a Sunday. It is very very cutting for colleagues who have to sit on a Committee in conditions of that character. When you work on a Committee and you have to take collective responsibility, there is a standard in the Trade Union Movement which we all follow. In this world loyalty to a decision gets less publicity than disloyalty under certain circumstances.

* * *

People have been on this platform today talking about the destruction of capitalism. The middle classes are not doing too badly as a whole under capitalism and Fascism. Lawyers and members of other professions have not done too badly. The thing that is being wiped out is the Trade Union Movement. It is the only defence that the workers have got. Our Internationals have been broken; our Austrian brothers tried to defend themselves. We did all that we could. It is we who are being wiped out and who will be wiped out if Fascism comes here—the last vestige of defence that it has taken over 100 years to build up. All the speeches that have been made against this resolution ought to have been made last year at Southport, and the people who oppose this resolution ought to have had the courage of their convictions and tabled the resolution at this Conference to the effect that we should withdraw from the League of Nations. You cannot be in and out at the same time, not if you are honest and that is the only thing that makes me question the honesty of some of them.

At Margate the T.U.C. was invited to a meeting of the three bodies to consider the logical consequence of last year's resolution at Southport which you carried. I wonder what sort of censure we would have heard today if we had failed at that moment? . . .

We went to Congress at Margate, and that resolution was carried by the joint meeting with three dissentients—the three Labour Peers who were present—everybody else in that meeting was absolutely unanimous. Cannot you understand me when I say, 'Do unto others as you would they should do unto you.' When you have been at a meeting of that character and have taken your decision, you have to stand to it and see it through. You are democrats. I can understand the Press outside dividing us, and the playing to the gallery that has been going on for the last few weeks. I feel bitter in my very soul about it, because if this Movement is going to win the country, when it is faced with a crisis it has got to give confidence that it is capable of coming to a decision.

When we went to the Trades Union Congress, Sir Walter Citrine was perfectly frank about sanctions. We were told that he ought not to have emphasised the military point. It is wrong to go to a Labour Congress and not to tell the whole truth. We went to Congress with the truth, and told Congress what it meant, and the result of the vote is known to you. Then, afterwards, we heard that there was a division. I feel that we have been let down. Every one of us on the General Council of the T.U.C. feel that we have been let down. We have had enough of it during the last ten or twelve years as Trade Union leaders— a very stiff time. I want to say to our friends who have joined us in this political Movement, that our predecessors formed this Party. It was not Keir Hardie who formed it, it grew out of the bowels of the Trades Union Congress. It was a struggle for status and equality, for Labour representation leading ultimately to power, and none of us have ever 'ratted'. Whether we have won or lost, we have taken our corner. We have never bothered much about whether we had place or power. Very few of us aspired to leadership. We have served on the National Council of Labour for the last four years. Arthur Henderson came to me and said: 'Do you think you can help me to revive the National Joint Council that has been put out of action? Do you think you can get a proper basis and help to renew the link that was broken in 1929?' We did it patiently in those four years. Every aspect of policy that the Labour Party wished to put up we have patiently examined, spending hours and hours of toil over it. What for? To make every Minister who goes into the next Labour Government efficient and effective so that he will not be left as before with no policy, whether it be foreign or domestic policy. We have striven for that, we have given of our best without hope of reward, no Parliamentary aspirant from the General Council on the Committee at all, but all of us willing to serve. And who am I to let my personality protrude as compared to this great Movement? Who is any man on that platform? I do sincerely ask this Conference to appreciate the Trade Unionist's position. Sir Stafford Cripps said there would be no split. He has done his best. (Voices, 'no, no'.) Oh, yes. Let me call attention to what has happened. He was elected a member of the Executive last year. I know nothing of what has happened in the Executive, but it is a most unusual thing to resign just prior to a Conference. If there was no intention to cast doubt upon it, he cast reflection upon the rest of us who took the responsibility when he was not present. It was cowardly to stab us in the back as he did by resigning and not going through. If he felt that the matter ought to have been reconsidered, why did not they call the body together again? Why did not they call us into consultation? The great crime of Ramsay MacDonald was that he never called in his Party and the crime of these people is that they have gone out, they have sown discord at the very moment when candidates want unity to face an Election. They have sown distrust and disunity at a moment when they could have called the body together again to consider whether or not there ought to be something done. We were left to get the news in the morning papers.

I ask any Trade Unionist: Have you ever found it in your own Union? Have we ever treated one another like that?

They say he who takes the sword shall perish by the sword. The man who has taken the sword is Mussolini, and because Mussolini has taken the sword we stand by the Scriptural doctrine and say that he shall perish by economic sanctions. I honestly believe in this Movement. I have shown you its history from the beginning, how its policy has been built up, how we have accepted responsibility, and pledged ourselves to the League, and I ask you to give tomorrow an almost unanimous vote, leaving it to those who cannot accept the policy of this great Conference to take their own course.

Note: At the end of the debate a card vote was taken. The result was as follows: In favour of the Resolution 2,168,000, Against 102,000, Majority for the Resolution 2,066,000.

The End of the Policy of Sanctions against Italy: On 3 October 1935 Italian forces invaded Abyssinia. The Council of the League of Nations condemned the Italian action and imposed economic sanctions upon Italy. This involved the member nations of the League in a ban on all imports from Italy and on some exports to Italy. The economic sanctions failed to stop the progress of the Italian armies. By May 1936 the Emperor of Abyssinia, Haile Selassie, was forced to leave his country and seek refuge in England and Mussolini proclaimed the annexation of Abyssinia as part of the Italian Empire. The failure of the League of Nations to deal effectively with Italian aggression in Abyssinia was a tremendous blow to the League's prestige and authority. It was evident that the policy of economic sanctions against Italy had proved completely ineffectual. In his speech to the House of Commons on 18 June 1936 Anthony Eden, who had succeeded Sir Samuel Hoare as Foreign Secretary, announced that the British Government would no longer impose these sanctions. The main points of his speech are given below.

(*29c*) *Extract from a speech of the Rt Hon Anthony Eden* (*Secretary of State for Foreign Affairs*) *in the House of Commons sitting as a Committee, 18 June 1936, on the subject of the British Government's proposals on the economic sanctions which had been imposed upon Italy* (Parliamentary Debates, House of Commons 1936 *5th series vol 313 cols 1200–1202*)

We have to admit that the purpose for which the sanctions were imposed has not been realised. It is not necessary to give a detailed account of the reasons for that fact; there are many. No doubt there were serious miscalculations. One of them was a miscalculation by military opinion in most countries that the conflict would last very much longer than it has in fact done, and that in consequence the sanctions which everyone knew could not operate at once, would produce their effect and assist thereby to obtain a settlement. In any event, I ask the Committee to remember that there was a very good reason for the League to enforce the sanctions, the particular ones they chose, because with an incomplete membership they were the only ones they could impose and which by their own action alone they could hope to see effective. . . . Oil could not be made effective by League action alone. . . .

The fact has to be faced that sanctions did not realise the purpose for which they were imposed. The Italian military campaign succeeded. The capital and the most important part of Abyssinia are in Italian military occupation, and so far as I am aware no Abyssinian Government survives in any part of the Emperor's territory. That is a situation which has got to be faced. . . .

Now I come to the steps to be taken at the next meeting of the League. The League, the Assembly of fifty nations there, will then have to review the whole situation of which this question of sanctions forms only a part. We cannot tell what will be the views of the various governments represented there, but His Majesty's Government, after mature consideration, on advice which I as Foreign Secretary thought it my duty to give them, have come to the conclusion that there is no longer any utility in continuing these measures as a means of pressure upon Italy. . . . It cannot be expected by anyone that the continuance of sanctions will restore in Abyssinia the position which has been destroyed; nobody expects that. That position can be restored only by military action. So far as I am aware no other government, certainly not this Government, is prepared to take such military action.

In my view sanctions can be maintained only for some clearly defined and specific purpose. The only such purpose conceivable is the restoration in Abyssinia of the position which has been destroyed. Since that restoration cannot be effected except by military action, I suggest that the purpose does not in fact exist, and to maintain sanctions without any clearly defined purpose which many people, I know, would wish to do—would have only this result: It would result in the crumbling of the sanctions front, so that in a few weeks' time the League would be confronted with a state of affairs still more derogatory than that which we have to face today. . . . I think it is right that the League should admit that sanctions have not realised their purpose and should face that fact. . . .

30. THE DEBATE ON
THE MUNICH AGREEMENT 1938

In an effort to obtain a peaceful solution to the crisis over Czechoslovakia, the Prime Minister, Neville Chamberlain, travelled to Munich and met Hitler on 29 September 1938. At this meeting, Chamberlain, Hitler, Daladier and Mussolini agreed upon the terms which were to be imposed upon the Czechs. On 30 September Chamberlain and Hitler had a private talk, as a result of which Hitler signed a statement renouncing warlike intentions against Great Britain and pledging himself to follow the method of consultation in any future question arising between the two countries.

Chamberlain returned to London on 1 October and was welcomed with tremendous enthusiasm. The Commons debate on the Munich Agreement lasted for four days (3 October to 6 October). Duff Cooper, the First Lord of the Admiralty, resigned in protest against the agreement and many speakers, most notably Winston Churchill, lamented the humiliation and weakness of Britain and the fate of Czechoslovakia. Many other members of Parliament supported Chamberlain and expressed their relief that Europe had been saved from war. The opposition to Chamberlain came from the Labour and Liberal parties and from some thirty Conservatives. Many of the Government's critics abstained from voting, however, and the motion approving the Munich Agreement was carried by 366 votes to 144.

EXTRACTS FROM THE SPEECHES OF THE PRIME MINISTER, (NEVILLE CHAMBERLAIN) AND WINSTON CHURCHILL

(*Parliamentary Debates, House of Commons, 1938* 5th series vol 339 cols 40–373)

3 October
The Prime Minister (Mr Chamberlain): When the House met last Wednesday, we were all under the shadow of a great and imminent menace. War, in a form more stark and terrible than ever before, seemed to be staring us in the face. Before I sat down, a message had come which gave us new hope that peace might yet be saved, and today, only a few days after,

we all meet in joy and thankfulness that the prayers of millions have been answered, and a cloud of anxiety has been lifted from our hearts. Upon the Members of the Cabinet the strain of the responsibility of these last few weeks has been almost overwhelming. Some of us, I have no doubt, will carry the mark of it for the rest of our days. Necessarily, the weight fell heavier upon some shoulders than others. While all bore their part, I would like here and now to pay an especial tribute of gratitude and praise to the man upon whom fell the first brunt of those decisions which had to be taken day by day almost hour by hour. The calmness, patience, and wisdom of the Foreign Secretary, and his lofty conception of his duty, not only to this country but to all humanity, were an example to us all, and sustained us all through the trials through which we have been passing. . . . After everything that has been said about the German Chancellor today and in the past, I do feel that the House ought to recognise the difficulty for a man in that position to take back such emphatic declarations as he had already made amidst the enthusiastic cheers of his supporters, and to recognise that in consenting, even though it were only at the last moment, to discuss with the representatives of other Powers those things which he had declared he had already decided once for all, was a real and a substantial contribution on his part. With regard to Signor Mussolini, his contribution was certainly notable and perhaps decisive. It was on his suggestion that the final stages of mobilisation were postponed for twenty-four hours to give us an opportunity of discussing the situation, and I wish to say that at the Conference itself both he and the Italian Foreign Secretary, Count Ciano, were most helpful in the discussions. It was they who, very early in the proceedings, produced the Memorandum which M. Daladier and I were able to accept as a basis of discussion. I think that Europe and the world have reason to be grateful to the head of the Italian Government for his work in contributing to a peaceful solution.

M. Daladier had in some respects the most difficult task of all four of us, because of the special relations uniting his country and Czechoslovakia, and I should like to say that his courage, his readiness to take responsibility, his pertinacity and his unfailing good humour were invaluable throughout the whole of our discussions. There is one other Power which was not represented at the Conference and which nevertheless we felt to be exercising a constantly increasing influence. I refer, of course, to the United States of America. Those messages of President Roosevelt, so firmly and yet so persuasively framed, showed how the voice of the most powerful nation in the world could make itself heard across 3,000 miles of ocean and sway the minds of men in Europe.

In my view the strongest force of all, one which grew and took fresh shapes and forms every day was the force not of any one individual, but was that unmistakable sense of unanimity among the peoples of the world that war somehow must be averted. The peoples of the British Empire were at one with those of Germany, of France and of Italy, and their anxiety, their intense desire for peace, pervaded the whole atmosphere of the conference, and I believe that that, and not threats, made possible the concessions that were made. I know the House will want to hear what I am sure it does not doubt, that throughout these discussions the Dominions, the Governments of the Dominions, have been kept in the closest touch with the march of events by telegraph and by personal contact, and I would like to say how greatly I was encouraged on each of the journeys I made to Germany by the knowledge that I went with the good wishes of the Governments of the Dominions. They shared all our anxieties and all our hopes. They rejoiced with us that peace was preserved, and with us they look forward to further efforts to consolidate what has been done.

Ever since I assumed my present office my main purpose has been to work for the pacification of Europe, for the removal of those suspicions and those animosities which have so long poisoned the air. The path which leads to appeasement is long and bristles with obstacles. The question of Czechoslovakia is the latest and perhaps the most dangerous. Now that we have got past it, I feel that it may be possible to make further progress along the road to sanity.

My right hon. Friend (Mr Duff Cooper) has alluded in somewhat bitter terms to my conversation last Friday morning with Herr Hitler. I do not know why that conversation should give rise to suspicion, still less to criticism. I entered into no pact. I made no new commitments. There is no secret understanding.

Our conversation was hostile to no other nation. The objects of that conversation, for which I asked, was to try to extend a little further the personal contact which I had established with Herr Hitler and which I believe to be essential in modern diplomacy. We had a friendly and entirely non-committal conversation, carried on, on my part, largely with a view to seeing whether there could be points in common between the head of a democratic Government and the ruler of a totalitarian State. We see the result in the declaration which has been published, in which my right hon. Friend finds so much ground for suspicion. What does it say?

There are three paragraphs. The first says that we agree:

'In recognising that the question of Anglo-German relations is of the first importance for the two countries and for Europe.'

Does anyone deny that? The second is an expression of opinion only. It says that:

'We regard the agreement signed last night and the Anglo-German Naval Agreement as symbolic of the desire of the two peoples never to go to war with one another again.'

Once more I ask, does anyone doubt that that is the desire of the two peoples? What is the last paragraph?

'We are resolved that the method of consultation shall be the method adopted to deal with any other questions that may concern our two countries, and we are determined to continue our efforts to remove possible sources of difference and thus to contribute to assure the peace of Europe.'

Who will stand up and condemn that sentence?

I believe there are many who will feel with me that such a declaration, signed by the German Chancellor and myself, is something more than a pious expression of opinion. In our relations with other countries everything depends upon there being sincerity and goodwill on both sides. I believe that there is sincerity and good will on both sides in this declaration. That is why to me its significance goes far beyond its actual words. If there is one lesson which we should learn from the events of these last weeks it is this, that lasting peace is not to be obtained by sitting still and waiting for it to come. It requires active, positive efforts to achieve it. No doubt I shall have plenty of critics who will say that I am guilty of facile optimism, and that I should disbelieve every word that is uttered by rulers of other great States in Europe. I am too much of a realist to believe that we are going to achieve our paradise in a day. We have only laid the foundations of peace. The superstructure is not even begun.

For a long period now we have been engaged in this country in a great programme of rearmament, which is daily increasing in pace and in volume. Let no one think that because we have signed this agreement between these four powers at Munich we can afford to relax our efforts in regard to that programme at this moment. Disarmament on the part of this country can never be unilateral again. We have tried that once, and we very nearly brought ourselves to disaster. If disarmament is to come it must come by steps, and it must come by the agreement and the active co-operation of other countries. Until we know that we have obtained that co-operation and until we have agreed upon the actual steps to be taken, we here must remain on guard.

*   *   *

5 October

Mr Churchill: If I do not begin this afternoon by paying the usual, and indeed almost invariable, tributes to the Prime Minister for his handling of this crisis, it is certainly not from any lack of personal regard. We have always, over a great many years, had very pleasant relations, and I have deeply understood from personal experiences of my own in a similar crisis the stress and strain he has had to bear; but I am sure it is much better to say exactly what we think about public affairs, and this is certainly not the time when it is worth anyone's while to court political popularity. . . . I will therefore, begin by saying the most unpopular and most unwelcome thing. I will begin by saying what everybody would like to ignore or forget but which must nevertheless be stated, namely, that we have sustained a total and unmitigated defeat, and that France has suffered even more than we have. . . . The utmost my right hon. Friend the Prime Minister has been able to secure by all his immense exertions, by all the great efforts and mobilisation which took place in this country, and by all the anguish and strain through which we have passed in this country, the utmost he has been able to gain—(Hon. Members: 'Is peace.') I thought I might be allowed to make that point in its due place, and I propose to deal with it. The utmost he has been able to gain for Czechoslovakia and in the matters which were in dispute has been that the German dictator, instead of snatching his victuals from the table, has been content to have them served to him course by course.

The Chancellor of the Exchequer said it was the first time Herr Hitler had been made to retract—I think that was the word—in any degree. We really must not waste time, after all this long Debate, upon the difference between the positions reached at Berchtesgaden, at Godesberg and at Munich. They can be very simply epitomised, if the House will permit me to vary the metaphor; £1 was demanded at pistol's point. When it was given, £2 were demanded at the pistol's point. Finally, the dictator consented to take £1 17s. 6d. and the rest in promises of goodwill for the future.

Now I come to the point, which was mentioned to me just now from some quarters of the House, about the saving of peace. No one has been a more resolute and uncompromising struggler for peace than the Prime Minister. Everyone knows that. Never has there been such intense and undaunted determination to maintain and to secure peace. That is quite true. Nevertheless, I am not quite clear why there was so much danger of Great Britain or France being involved in a war with Germany at this juncture if, in fact, they were ready all along to sacrifice Czechoslovakia. The terms which the Prime Minister brought back with him—I quite agree at the last moment; everything had got off the rails and nothing but his intervention could have saved the peace, but I am talking of the events of the summer—could easily have been agreed, I believe, through the ordinary diplomatic channels at any time during the summer. And I will say this, that I believe the Czechs, left to themselves and told they were going to get no help from the Western Powers, would have been able to make better terms than they have got—they could hardly have worse—after all this tremendous perturbation.

* * *

I venture to think that in future the Czechoslovak State cannot be maintained as an independent entity. You will find that in a period of time which may be measured by years, but may be measured only by months, Czechoslovakia will be engulfed in the Nazi régime. Perhaps they may join it in despair or in revenge. At any rate, that story is over and told. But we cannot consider the abandonment and ruin of Czechoslovakia in the light only of what happened only last month. It is the most grievous consequence which we have yet experienced of what we have done and of what we have left undone in the last five years—five years of futile good intention, five years of eager search for the line of least resistance, five years of uninterrupted retreat of British power, five years of neglect of our air defences. Those are the features which I stand here to declare and which marked an improvident stewardship for which Great Britain and France have dearly to pay. We have been reduced in those five years from a position of security so overwhelming and so unchallengeable that we never cared to think about it. We have been reduced from a position where the very word 'war' was considered one which would be used only by persons qualifying for a lunatic asylum. We have been reduced from a position of safety and power—power to do good, power to be generous to a beaten foe, power to make terms with Germany, power to give her proper redress for her grievances, power to stop her arming if we chose, power to take any step in strength or mercy or justice which we thought right—reduced in five years from a position safe and unchallenged to where we stand now.

When I think of the fair hopes of a long peace which still lay before Europe at the beginning of 1933 when Herr Hitler first obtained power, and of all the opportunities of arresting the growth of the Nazi power which have been thrown away, when I think of the immense combinations and resources which have been neglected or squandered, I cannot believe that a parallel exists in the whole course of history. So far as this country is concerned the responsibility must rest with those who have the undisputed control of our political affairs. They neither prevented Germany from rearming, nor did they rearm ourselves in time. They quarrelled with Italy without saving Ethiopia. They exploited and discredited the vast institution of the League of Nations and they neglected to make alliances and combinations which might have repaired previous errors, and thus they left us in the hour of trial without adequate national defence or effective international security.

What I find unendurable is the sense of our country falling into the power, into the orbit and influence of Nazi Germany, and of our existence becoming dependent upon their good will or pleasure. It is to prevent that that I have tried my best to urge the maintenance of every bulwark of defence—first the timely creation of an Air Force superior to anything within striking distance of our shores; secondly, the gathering together of the collective strength of many nations; and thirdly, the making of alliances and military conventions, all within the Covenant, in order to gather together forces at any rate to restrain the onward movement of this Power. It has all been in vain. Every position has been successively undermined and abandoned on specious and plausible excuses. We do not want to be led upon the high road to becoming a satellite of the German Nazi system of European domination. In a very few years, perhaps in a very few months, we shall be confronted with demands with which we shall no doubt be invited to comply. Those demands may affect the surrender of territory or the surrender of liberty. I foresee and foretell that the policy of submission will carry with it restrictions upon the freedom of speech and debate in Parliament, on public platforms, and discussions in the Press, for it will be said—indeed, I hear it said sometimes now—that we cannot allow the Nazi system of dictatorship to be criticised by ordinary, common English politicians. Then, with a Press under control, in part direct but more potently indirect, with every organ of public opinion doped and chloroformed into acquiescence, we shall be conducted along further stages of our journey.

*   *   *

I do not grudge our loyal brave people, who were ready to do their duty no matter what the cost, who never flinched under the strain of last week—I do not grudge them the natural, spontaneous outburst of joy and relief when they learned that the hard ordeal would no longer be required of them at the moment; but they should know the truth. They should know that there has been gross neglect and deficiency in our defences; they should know that we have sustained a defeat without a war, the consequences of which will travel far with us along our road; they should know that we have passed an awful milestone in our history, when the whole equilibrium of Europe has been deranged, and that the terrible words have for the time being been pronounced against the Western democracies: 'Thou art weighed in the balance and found wanting.' And do not suppose that this is the end. This is only the beginning of the reckoning. This is only the first sip, the first foretaste of a bitter cup which will be proffered to us year by year unless by a supreme recovery of moral health and martial vigour, we arise again and take our stand for freedom as in the olden time.

31. THE OUTBREAK OF WAR 1939

The following extracts are from speeches made in the House of Commons on 1, 2 and 3 September 1939. Sir Archibald Sinclair was the leader of the Liberal Party and Arthur Greenwood was acting as leader of the Labour Party in place of Clement Attlee who was ill. It was when Greenwood rose to speak on 2 September that Leopold Amery, a Conservative critic of the Government, shouted to him 'Speak for England'. This well-known interruption was not recorded in the Official Report.

Before Chamberlain addressed the House of Commons at 12.6 p.m. on 3 September he had already broadcast to the nation at 11.15 a.m. and announced that Britain was at war with Germany.

THE OUTBREAK OF WAR, SEPTEMBER 1939

(*Parliamentary Debates, House of Commons, 1938–39* 5th series
vol 351)

Friday, 1 September 1939

German Attack on Poland

6.5.p.m.

The Prime Minister (Mr Chamberlain): I do not propose to say many words tonight. The time has come when action rather than speech is required. Eighteen months ago in this House I prayed that the responsibility might not fall upon me to ask this country to accept the awful arbitrament of war. I fear that I may not be able to avoid that responsibility. But, at any rate, I cannot wish for conditions in which such a burden should fall upon me in which I should feel clearer than I do today as to where my duty lies. No man can say that the Government could have done more to try to keep open the way for an honourable and equitable settlement of the dispute between Germany and Poland. Nor have we neglected any means of making it crystal clear to the German Government that if they insisted on using force again in the manner in which they had used it in the past we were resolved to oppose them by force. Now that all the relevant documents are being made public we shall stand at the bar of history knowing that the responsibility for this terrible catastrophe lies on the shoulders of one man—the German Chancellor, who has not hesitated to plunge the world into misery in order to serve his own senseless ambition.

(After outlining the efforts which had been made to bring about a peaceful settlement of the dispute, the Prime Minister announced that German troops had invaded Poland that morning).

In these circumstances there is only one course open to us. His Majesty's Ambassador in Berlin and the French Ambassador have been instructed to hand to the German Government the following document:

'Early this morning the German Chancellor issued a proclamation to the German army which indicated clearly that he was to attack Poland. Information which has reached His Majesty's Government in the United Kingdom and the French Government indicates that German troops have crossed the Polish frontier and that attacks upon Polish towns are proceeding. In these circumstances it appears to the Governments of the United Kingdom and of France that by their action the German Government have created conditions, namely, an aggressive act of force against Poland threatening the independence of Poland, which call for the implementation by the Governments of the United Kingdom and of France of the undertaking to Poland to come to her assistance. I am accordingly to inform your Excellency that unless the German Government are prepared to give His Majesty's Government satisfactory assurances that the German Government have suspended all aggressive action against Poland and are prepared promptly to withdraw their forces from Polish territory, His Majesty's Government in the United Kingdom will without hesitation fulfil their obligations to Poland.'

... If a reply to this last warning is unfavourable, and I do not suggest that it is likely to be otherwise, His Majesty's Ambassador is instructed to ask for his passports. In that case we are ready. Yesterday, we took further steps towards the completion of our defensive preparations. This morning we ordered complete mobilisation of the whole of the Royal Navy, Army and Royal Air Force. ...

It now only remains for us to set our teeth and to enter upon this struggle, which we ourselves earnestly endeavoured to avoid, with determination to see it through to the end. We shall enter it with a clear conscience, with the support of the Dominions and the British Empire, and the moral approval of the greater part of the world. We have no quarrel with the German people, except that they allow themselves to be governed by a Nazi Government. As long as that Government exists and pursues the methods it has so persistently followed during the last two years, there will be no peace in Europe. We shall merely pass from one crisis to another, and see one country after another attacked by methods which have now become familiar to us in their sickening technique. We are resolved that these methods must come to an end. If out of the struggle we again re-establish in the world the rules of good faith and the renunciation of force, why, then even the sacrifices that will be entailed upon us will find their fullest justification.

Saturday, 2 September 1939

Germany and Poland, Italian Proposals

7.44 p.m.

The Prime Minister (Mr Chamberlain): Sir Nevile Henderson was received by Herr von Ribbentrop at half-past nine last night, and he delivered the warning which was read to the House yesterday. Herr von Ribbentrop replied that he must submit the communication to the German Chancellor. Our Ambassador declared his readiness to receive the Chancellor's reply. Up to the present no reply has been received.

It may be that the delay is caused by consideration of a proposal which, meanwhile, had been put forward by the Italian Government, that hostilities should cease and that there should then immediately be a conference between the Five Powers, Great Britain, France, Poland, Germany and Italy. While appreciating the efforts of the Italian Government, His Majesty's Government, for their part, would find it impossible to take part in a conference while Poland is being subjected to invasion, her towns are under bombardment and Danzig is being made the subject of a unilateral settlement by force. His Majesty's Government will, as stated yesterday, be bound to take action unless the German forces are withdrawn from Polish territory. They are in communication with the French Government as to the limit of time within which it would be necessary for the British and French Governments to know whether the German Government were prepared to effect such a withdrawal. If the German Government should agree to withdraw their forces then His Majesty's Government would be willing to regard the position as being the same as it was before German forces crossed the Polish frontier. That is to say, the way would be open to discussion between the German and Polish Governments on the matters at issue between them, on the understanding that the settlement arrived at was one that safeguarded the vital interests of Poland and was secured by an international guarantee. If the German and Polish Governments wished that other Powers should be associated with them in the discussion, His Majesty's Government for their part would be willing to agree.

There is one other matter to which allusion should be made in order that the present situation may be perfectly clear. Yesterday Herr Förster who, on 23 August, had, in contravention of the Danzig constitution, become the head of the State, decreed the incorporation of Danzig in the Reich and the dissolution of the constitution. Herr Hitler was asked to give effect to this decree by German law. At a meeting of the Reichstag yesterday morning a law was passed for the reunion of Danzig with the Reich. The international status of Danzig as a Free City is established by a treaty of which His Majesty's Government are a signatory, and the Free City was placed under the protection of the League of Nations. The rights given to Poland in Danzig by treaty are defined and confirmed by agreement concluded between Danzig and Poland. The action taken by the Danzig authorities and the Reichstag yesterday is the final step in the unilateral repudiation of these international instruments, which could only be modified by negotiation. His Majesty's Government do not, therefore, recognise either the validity of the grounds on which the action of the Danzig authorities was based, the validity of this action itself, or of the effect given to it by the German Government.

7.48 p.m.
Mr Greenwood: This is indeed a grave moment. I believe the whole House is perturbed by the right hon. Gentleman's statement. There is a growing feeling, I believe, in all quarters of the

House that this incessant strain must end sooner or later—and, in a sense, the sooner the better. But if we are to march, I hope we shall march in complete unity, and march with France . . . I am speaking under very difficult circumstances with no opportunity to think about what I should say; and I speak what is in my heart at this moment. I am gravely disturbed. An act of aggression took place thirty-eight hours ago. The moment that act of aggression took place one of the most important treaties of modern times automatically came into operation. There may be reasons why instant action was not taken. I am not prepared to say—and I have tried to play a straight game—I am not prepared to say what I would have done if I had been one of those sitting on those Benches. That delay may have been justifiable, but there are many of us on all sides of this House who view with the gravest concern the fact that hours went by and news came in of bombing operations, and news today of an intensification of it, and I wonder how long we are prepared to vacillate at a time when Britain and all that Britain stands for, and human civilisation, are in peril. We must march with the French. I hope these words of mine may go further. I do not believe that the French dare at this juncture go, or would dream at this juncture of going back on the sacred oaths that they have taken. It is not for me to rouse any kind of suspicion—and I would never dream of doing so at this time, but if, as the right hon. Gentleman has told us, deeply though I regret it, we must wait upon our Allies, I should have preferred the Prime Minister to have been able to say tonight definitely: 'It is either peace or war.'

Tomorrow we meet at 12. I hope the Prime Minister then—well he must be in a position to make some further statement. (Hon. Members: 'Definite'). And I must put this point to him. Every minute's delay now means the loss of life, imperilling our national interests—

Mr Boothby: Honour.

Mr Greenwood: Let me finish my sentence. I was about to say imperilling the very foundations of our national honour, and I hope, therefore, that tomorrow morning, however hard it may be to the right hon. Gentleman—and no one would care to be in his shoes tonight—we shall know the mind of the British Government, and that there shall be no more devices for dragging out what has been dragged out too long. The moment we look like weakening, at that moment dictatorship knows we are beaten. We shall not be beaten. We cannot be beaten; but delay is dangerous, and I hope the Prime Minister—it is very difficult to press him too hard at this stage—will be able to tell us when the House meets at noon tomorrow what the final decision is, and whether then our promises are in process of fulfilment, for in my mind there can be no escape now from the dilemma into which we have been placed. I cannot see Herr Hitler, in honesty, making any deal which he will not be prepared to betray. Therefore, thinking very hurriedly in these few moments, I believe that the die is cast, and we want to know in time.

7.56 p.m.

Sir Archibald Sinclair: This meeting will not have been held in vain if it demonstrates to the world that the British Parliament will not tolerate delay in the fulfilment of our honourable obligations to Poland. The Prime Minister in his statement said that we have received no reply from the German Government to our Note, and that the delay in sending us a reply might have been caused by consideration of the Italian proposal for a conference. Consideration of that proposal has, at any rate, caused no delay in the advance of the German Army, and I am sure that Parliament feels that a reply must be demanded, unless the advance of those armies is promptly stopped. It is, of course, vital that we should march in step with our French allies. Let not the confidence which we feel in our French allies waver if, indeed, they wish to await the decision of their Chamber. That requirement may impose some measure of delay at this time, but the Prime Minister has undertaken to make a statement at noon tomorrow. I hope that before then some information of this sitting of Parliament and of the feeling of Parliament on this issue may be conveyed to the French Government. I have no doubt that their response will be generous and cordial and that their feelings will be the same as ours, but it is well that they should know what ours are. I hope that when we meet at noon tomorrow the Prime Minister will be able to give us a statement.

Sunday, 3 September 1939

12.6 p.m.

The Prime Minister (Mr Chamberlain): When I spoke last

night to the House I could not but be aware that in some parts of the House there were doubts and some bewilderment as to whether there had been any weakening, hesitation or vacillation on the part of His Majesty's Government. In the circumstances, I make no reproach, for if I had been in the same position as hon. Members not sitting on this Bench and not in possession of all the information which we have, I should very likely have felt the same. The statement which I have to make this morning will show that there were no grounds for doubt. We were in consultation all day yesterday with the French Government and we felt that the intensified action which the Germans were taking against Poland allowed no delay in making our own position clear. Accordingly, we decided to send to our Ambassador in Berlin instructions which he was to hand at nine o'clock this morning to the German Foreign Secretary and which read as follows:

'Sir,

In the communication which I had the honour to make to you on 1 September, I informed you, on the instructions of His Majesty's Principal Secretary of State for Foreign Affairs, that unless the German Government were prepared to give His Majesty's Government in the United Kingdom satisfactory assurances that the German Government had suspended all aggressive action against Poland and were prepared promptly to withdraw their forces from Polish territory, His Majesty's Government in the United Kingdom would, without hesitation, fulfil their obligations to Poland.

Although this communication was made more than twenty-four hours ago, no reply has been received, but German attacks upon Poland have been continued and intensified. I have, accordingly, the honour to inform you that unless not later than 11 a.m., British Summer Time, today, 3 September, satisfactory assurances to the above effect have been given by the German Government and have reached His Majesty's Government in London, a state of war will exist between the two countries as from that hour.'

That was the final note. No such undertaking was received by the time stipulated, and, consequently, this country is at war with Germany. I am in a position to inform the House that, according to arrangements made between the British and

French Governments, the French Ambassador in Berlin is at this moment making a similar *démarche*, accompanied also by a definite time limit. The House has already been made aware of our plans. As I said the other day, we are ready.

This is a sad day for all of us, and to none is it sadder than to me. Everything that I have worked for, everything that I have hoped for, everything that I have believed in during my public life, has crashed into ruins. There is only one thing left for me to do; that is, to devote what strength and powers I have to forwarding the victory of the cause for which we have to sacrifice so much. I cannot tell what part I may be allowed to play myself; I trust I may live to see the day when Hitlerism has been destroyed and a liberated Europe has been re-established.